SELEC

PHOVIOU   AT   END   OF   INTCHYIGNS.

THE SACRAMENTS
AND THE MYSTERY OF CHRIST

Fr Francis Selman

The Sacraments and the Mystery of Christ

FAMILY PUBLICATIONS • MARYVALE INSTITUTE

ISBN 9781871217926

published by
Family Publications
Denis Riches House, 66 Sandford Lane
Kennington, Oxford OX1 5RP

www.familypublications.co.uk

and by

Maryvale Institute
Maryvale House, Old Oscott Hill
Birmingham B44 9AG

www.maryvale.ac.uk

Printed in Lithuania through
s|s|media ltd

Contents

To Philip Trower

'The fact that the Church is the "universal sacrament of salvation" shows how the sacramental economy ultimately determines the way that Christ, the one Saviour, through the Spirit, reaches our lives in all their particularity. The Church receives and at the same time expresses what she herself is in the seven sacraments, thanks to which God's grace concretely influences the lives of the faithful, so that their whole existence, redeemed by Christ, can become an act of worship pleasing to God.'

– Pope Benedict XVI, *Sacramentum Caritatis*

Preface

This book provides an introduction to the sacraments, which combines a general view of the sacraments, in the first part, with individual chapters on the seven sacraments in the second part. The book is based on the course on the sacraments which I give to students at Maryvale Institute, who come from many walks of life and are living and working in ordinary parishes. The present book is thus directed to anyone interested in deepening their knowledge and awareness of their Christian faith and of how the life and worship of the Church relate us to Christ. I also hope that this book may provide ready material for catechists and preachers who have to teach or preach about the sacraments.

My approach to the sacraments is to see them as the way we participate in the mysteries of Christ's life, death and resurrection, which bring us healing and new life. Christ came down to us on earth, so that we 'may have life, and have it to the full' (Jn 10:10). The life of Christ is now in us by the inner working of the Holy Spirit, who raised up Jesus from the dead (cf. Rom 8:11). We receive the life of the risen Christ through the sacraments. Indeed, as Francis Xavier Durrwell said in a book which attracted many readers when it appeared in English translation in the 1960s, the Easter mystery opens out to us in the sacraments (*The Resurrection*, p.332). Thus, like St Paul, we come 'to know Christ and the power of his resurrection' (Phil 3:10) through the sacraments.

How does this book differ from other books on the seven sacraments? First, it includes references to recent papal encyclicals which do not occur in standard books written before the year 2000. Secondly, I have made considerable use of the Irish Dominican, Fr Colman O'Neill, who I think deserves to be better known. What I like about Colman O'Neill's approach to the sacraments is the way it focuses on the whole mystery of Christ. Although I freely use the book *Christ the Sacrament* of another Dominican, Edward Schillebeeckx, this does not mean that I approve of everything that Schillebeeckx subsequently wrote. But this book of his seems to me to represent faithfully the teaching of St Thomas Aquinas. St Thomas himself drew considerably from the Fathers of the Church in his writing on the sacraments. And the Fathers of the Church, in their catechetical instructions and homilies, show that they saw the sacraments especially as the means by which we participate in the mysteries of Christ's life, death and resurrection. It is worth recalling that the authors of the *Catechism of the Catholic Church* were influenced by the books of men like Colman O'Neill, writing in the 1960s, when they were students of theology. Thus, thought which appeared to be quite new at the time passes into the tradition of the Church.

The numbering of the Psalms is that of the Vulgate edition of the Bible. The quotations from scripture are taken from the Revised Standard Version, except where I make my own translations of passages in the New Testament.

F.J. Selman
March 2009

Abbreviations

CCC   *Catechism of the Catholic Church* (1992).
DS   Denzinger-Schönmetzer, *Enchiridion Symbolorum et Definitionum*, 34th edition.
LG   Second Vatican Council, *Lumen Gentium* (Constitution on the Church).
ND   Neuner-Dupuis, *The Christian Faith*.
PL   Migne, *Patrologia Latina*.
SC   Second Vatican Council, *Sacrosanctum Concilium* (Constitution on the Sacred Liturgy).
ST   Thomas Aquinas, St, *Summa Theologiae*.

PART ONE: INTRODUCTION

Chapter One

The Trinity and Incarnation

The sacraments are means by which the grace of God comes to us through Christ and his mystical body, the Church, conforming us with the saving mysteries of Christ's life, death and resurrection. In order to understand the sacraments, then, we first need to see them in relation to the other great mysteries of the Christian faith. The sacraments are founded on the incarnation, and the incarnation takes us back to the Trinity, the fountain of all the mysteries of salvation, for the Son was sent into the world by the Father and the human nature which the Son united to himself was conceived by the power of the Holy Spirit in the womb of Mary. As Fr Paul Haffner says, the sacraments are rooted in the mystery of the Trinity, for they are the means by which Christ, who came forth from the Father in coming into the world as man, still acts in us by his Holy Spirit.[1] The Holy Spirit continues to act in the Church as he was visibly sent down on the Church at Pentecost.

The purpose of the whole plan, or economy, of salvation, the *Catechism of the Catholic Church* tells us, is to bring human beings to share in the life of the Trinity.[2] The end for which we have been made is to have communion with

1. *The Sacramental Mystery*, pp.1f.
2. CCC 260.

the blessed Trinity. St John writes of this communion with the Trinity when he says, 'we proclaim to you what we have seen and heard, so that you may have communion (*koinonia*) with us; and our communion is with the Father and with his Son Jesus Christ' (1 Jn 1:3). With the Father and the Son, we can also understand their Love, the Holy Spirit, who is inseparable from them. The way by which we come to God is through Jesus Christ, in whom human nature is united to divine nature: 'no one comes to the Father except through me' (Jn 14:6). And the way we are joined to Christ is through his mystical body, the Church. Grace comes to us from the Trinity through the humanity of Christ, which is a source of grace for us as it is united to his divine nature. We thus receive grace through the humanity of Christ as we are like branches which draw their life-giving sap from the vine stock. Christ expresses this relation when he says, 'I am the vine, you are the branches' (Jn 15:5).

Our communion with God, however, is a *personal* communion, because God is three Persons; the Father, the Son, and the Holy Spirit. But we can only have personal communion with God, as the Flemish Dominican father Edward Schillebeeckx notes, through *grace*.[3] By our natural powers we only know God as he is One through the works of creation, but not as the Trinity. All grace comes to us through the humanity of Christ, since human nature is

---

3. *Christ the Sacrament*, p.2. The title of this book in the original is 'Christ the Sacrament of Encounter with God's Son' (*Sacrament van de Godsontmoeting*). By leaving out 'Encounter', the English title misses the whole point of Schillebeeckx's book.

united to divine nature in him. The divine Word, who became flesh by uniting human nature to himself in the incarnation, is 'full of grace and truth' (Jn 1:14). Thus we are not just saved by the Word but by the Word *made flesh,* through the humanity of Christ joined to his divine nature, which is the spring of grace.

Christ is the Mediator between God and human beings, indeed the only Mediator, because he is God and man in one person. As St Paul says, the Mediator is 'the man (*anthropos*) Christ Jesus' (1 Tim 2:5). The question for Edward Schillebeeckx was: How can we come to God the Trinity through the humanity of Christ when he has withdrawn his body from the Earth by his ascension into heaven? Or, to put this slightly differently: How can we have bodily contact with Christ, as the men and women who met him when he lived on earth could touch him, now that his body is glorified and seated at the right hand of the Father in heaven? The answer lies in the sacraments: just as power went out of Jesus when the woman with a flow of blood touched the hem of his garment (Lk 8:46), so divine power enters us through the sacraments. The nineteenth-century German theologian, Matthias Scheeben, says that power really flows through the sacraments as it did through Christ's outward actions.[4] Just as the Son of God acted as man through his body on earth and sometimes touched those whom he healed, so he continues to act for our salvation through his mystical body, the Church. And just as Christ cast out demons and so healed people 'by the Spirit of God' (Mt 12:28), so he continues to heal us by the

4. *The Mysteries of Christianity*, pp.570f.

action of the Holy Spirit though the sacraments. Christ's power continues to reach us through the sacraments because these are, so to speak, the actions of his body, the Church. Every celebration of a sacrament, the Catechism tells us, is 'an encounter between Christ and the Church',[5] just as in every miracle that Christ performed there was an encounter between him and a person with faith, whom he healed.

Our encounter with other persons in this life is through the body. All human communication in this life is bodily. For example, we communicate our thoughts by expressing them with words which we utter with our mouths and have learnt from others by hearing them with our ears. In the same way, as we are not just spirit but body as well, our contact with Christ is not just spiritual by faith but also *corporeal* through the sacraments. St John speaks of the Word of Life as that 'which we have seen with our eyes, which we have looked upon and touched with our hands' (1 Jn 1:1). We now have personal encounter with Christ through the *visible, audible, tangible* signs of the sacraments. In this way, the sacraments can be seen as encounters with Christ through signs which we perceive with the senses of touching, seeing and hearing, as the sacraments consist of material elements, action and words. We should not, however, just think of sacraments as personal 'encounters' with Christ but also retain the common view of them as signs of God's transforming grace.

Ever since the incarnation, the way for us to encounter God and have communion with the Trinity has been through Jesus Christ, who is the Son of God and man.

---

5. CCC 1097.

The way we come to God the Trinity is through receiving the sacraments, Schillebeeckx says, because we encounter Christ in the sacraments, who is the way to the Father.[6] Christ himself is personally God and personally man. He is personally God because he is the Second Person of the Trinity; he is personally man because this divine person, who existed from eternity, united a complete human nature, like ours in every way except for sin, to himself in the unity of his person. As the Council of Chalcedon declared in 451: 'each of the two natures (divine and human) was preserved as they came together in one person (*prosopon*) and one hypostasis'. To meet Jesus when he lived on earth was thus to meet God, for Jesus is God who lived on earth in visible, human form. As Jesus said to Philip, 'Whoever has seen me has seen the Father' (Jn 14:9). When we meet Christ in the sacraments, therefore, we also encounter God and have communion with the Trinity.

We also have personal communion with the Trinity because the Holy Trinity dwells in us: 'If anyone loves me, he will keep my word, and the Father will love him, and we will come to him and make our dwelling with him' (Jn 14:23). The Father and the Son of course include the Holy Spirit who is their Love, proceeding from them. This doctrine of the indwelling of the Trinity is a rather forgotten one but one of the great realities of our lives, provided that we are in the state of grace. The indwelling of the Trinity is especially an effect of the sacrament of the Eucharist for it follows that when we are in Christ and Christ is in us through communion, and as he is in the

---

6. *Christ the Sacrament*, p.5.

Father and the Father is in him, the Father and the Son are in us together with their Holy Spirit.

Almost contemporary with Fr Schillebeeckx, another Dominican, Colman O'Neill, who taught at Fribourg in Switzerland, produced a book presenting the sacraments in a similar way as an encounter with Christ. Schillebeeckx published his book in 1960, just before the Second Vatican Council, Colman O'Neill during the Council in 1964. Starting with God, O'Neill said that, through the incarnation, God encounters us in a human way through the humanity of his Son.[7] Those who meet Jesus in the Gospels had contact with One who was God and man: they could touch him and were touched by him. For example, Jesus touched the eyes of the man born-blind (Jn 9:6). Now we continue to touch Christ through the sacraments. As St Thomas Aquinas frequently says, we 'touch' God by faith and the sacraments.[8] We touch Christ through the sacraments because they have the same structure as the Word incarnate: as Christ is the Word who united to himself a visible, tangible body, so a sacrament consists of a sensible sign with a word joined to it.[9] Indeed, the sacraments are an extension of the incarnation which has not ceased with Christ's bodily departure from the Earth at his ascension but continues forever in heaven, where his risen and glorified body is an enduring reality. As Schillebeeckx says, the sacraments are an extension of 'the body of the Lord' and a prolongation of Christ's glorified

---

7. *Meeting Christ in the Sacraments*, p.88.
8. ST 3a 49, 3 ad 1.
9. Ibid., 3a 60, 6.

bodiliness.[10] We find the same thought in Fr John Saward, a writer of undoubted orthodoxy: 'The Sacraments are an extension of the incarnation'.[11] As the Son of God touched those whom he cured, so he now touches and heals us through the sacraments, in which there is seeing, touching and hearing. The sacraments are, as it were, the hands of the glorified Christ, extended in space and time, in order to touch and thus to heal, to sanctify, and thereby to deify the wounded sons of Adam'.[12] We find the same view in Colman O'Neill, who said that the sacraments are extensions of Christ's humanity, which bring men and women to the saving power of Christ's mysteries.[13]

---

10. Op. cit., pp.41, 44.
11. *Cradle of Redeeming Love*, p.97.
12. Ibid., p.97.
13. *Meeting Christ in the Sacraments*, p.66.

Chapter Two
Sharing in the Mysteries of Christ

The mysteries of Christ's life are the foundation of the sacraments. St Leo the Great said, 'what was visible in our Redeemer has passed over into the sacraments'.[14] In other words, what Christ worked by his miracles of healing, life, death and resurrection is now effective for us through the sacraments. The Catechism states: 'The mysteries of Christ's life are the foundations of what he would henceforth dispense in the sacraments'.[15] Indeed, 'Christ's whole life is a mystery of redemption'.[16] Schillebeeckx sees all Christ's saving activity as sacramental because Christ is God, who acted in a human way: God's saving acts were realized in human form in Jesus.[17]

We are not just saved by the Paschal mystery of Christ's death and resurrection but by *all* the events of his life, which were all saving because they all, in one way or another, led up to and foreshadowed his passion and death. For example, the Presentation of Jesus in the Temple when he

---

14. *Sermo* 74, 2 (*De Ascensione* 2, 2) PL 54, 398. This quotation has not been accurately translated in the Catechism, which substitutes 'Saviour' for *Redentore* and 'mysteries' for *sacramentis* (CCC 1115).
15. CCC 1115.
16. CCC 517.
17. Op. cit., p.15.

was 40 days old clearly prefigured the offering of his body on the cross. The miracles of healing which he worked on the Sabbath led to his death, because they aroused the anger of the chief priests and Pharisees who resolved to kill him. The miracles by which Jesus cast out demons pointed toward his crucifixion, when he overcame the power of the Devil. Referring to the time when he would be lifted up on the cross, Jesus said: 'now shall the ruler of this world be cast out' (Jn 12:31). All Christ's actions and sufferings as man are saving in virtue of his divine nature, to which his humanity was, and still is, united. As St Thomas Aquinas neatly puts it, what Christ suffered in the body has spiritual power because of the divinity to which his body was united.[18] Jesus' acts as man are also saving, because his human nature was sanctified by the Holy Spirit. As St Thomas again says, 'the salvation of the human race is perfected by the incarnation of the Son and the gift of the Holy Spirit'.[19] His human nature was conceived by the power of the Holy Spirit, and the Holy Spirit came down visibly on Christ at his baptism in the River Jordan, although he was already full of the Holy Spirit, as a sign that the Holy Spirit would sanctify our human nature in baptism. The Holy Spirit was poured out on the Church when Christ's humanity had been glorified, again by the Holy Spirit, with the completion of the Paschal mystery at Pentecost. Thus the Holy Spirit was at work in all the mysteries of Christ, from the moment of his incarnation at the Annunciation to his sending of the Spirit on the Church at Pentecost. All Christ's acts

---

18. ST 3a 48, 6 ad 2.
19. ST 1a 32, 1 ad 3.

as man have power to save us, because Christ possessed the fullness of grace in his human nature: he is the Word made flesh, who is 'full of grace and truth' (Jn 1:14). Thus his humanity is a source of grace for others: 'And from his fullness we have received, grace upon grace' (Jn 1:18).

Schillebeeckx divides the mystery of salvation by Christ into four stages:

1. The Incarnation (the sending of the Son by the Trinity).
2. The Passion of Christ (his obedience until death).
3. The Resurrection and Ascension (the exaltation of Jesus).
4. Pentecost (the sending of the Holy Spirit).

We first notice from this scheme that the mysteries of Christ are encompassed by the revelation of the Trinity with the sending of the Son by the Father and the sending of the Holy Spirit by the Father and the Son. Secondly, the second, third and fourth stages make up the Paschal mystery, which was completed with the sending of the Holy Spirit on the Church. Schillebeeckx says that we encounter Christ in the mysteries of the Passover and Pentecost in the sacraments;[20] in the mystery of Pentecost, because, as Schillebeeckx notes, all the sacraments include in their rite an invocation of the Holy Spirit. But Christ could only send the Holy Spirit when his body had been glorified: 'for as yet the spirit had not been given, because Jesus was not yet glorified' (Jn 7:39).[21] It was the *risen* Christ

---

20. Op. cit., p.45.
21. Cf. F.X. Durrwell, *The Resurrection*, pp.82-83. Durrwell shows that the source of the living water in Jn 7:38 is Christ, not the believer.

who sent down the Holy Spirit: 'Being therefore exalted at the right hand of God, and having received from the Father the promise of the Holy Spirit, he has poured out this which you see and hear' (Acts 2:33). Thus the sending of the Holy Spirit (stage 4) presupposed the glorifying of Jesus (stage 3). Stage 4 required stage 3, because Christ's humanity could only become the source of the Spirit when he had overcome death by rising from the dead.

Each of the four stages outlined by Schillebeeckx requires the previous one. Pentecost required the ascension, as Jesus told his disciples that it was good that he would leave them and return to his Father, otherwise he could not send the Holy Spirit (Jn 14:16; 16:14). But Jesus could not be exalted by his resurrection and ascension unless he first lowered himself by his suffering and death: 'he humbled himself and became obedient unto death, even death on a cross. Therefore God has highly exalted him' (Phil 2:8-9). Jesus became the source of salvation by his passion: 'Although he was Son, he learned obedience through suffering; and being made perfect he became the source of eternal salvation to all who obey him' (Hebr 5:8-9). The second stage naturally required the first of the incarnation, because the Son took a human body so that he could suffer for us, offer his body to the Father, and so take away our sins.

Conversely, moving forwards and upwards, the second stage required the third, because Christ's death only became the source of Salvation for us as it was followed by the resurrection. The cross was only made effective by the resurrection.[22] Although there is no forgiveness of sins

---

22. Ibid., p.33.

without the cross, equally, as St Paul remarks, without the resurrection we would still be in our sins (1 Cor 15:17). Christ's death was redemptive precisely because it resulted in the resurrection.[23] The nineteenth-century theologian, Matthias Scheeben, pointed out that Christ's sacrifice only endures eternally in heaven because of the resurrection.[24] God accepted the sacrifice of his Son when he took his body and entered the heavenly sanctuary by his ascension; 'But when Christ had offered for all time a single sacrifice for sins, he sat down at the right hand of God' (Hebr 10:12). We may also note that by Christ's entry into heaven as man at his ascension, heaven once again became a place open for us to enter.[25]

Schillebeeckx discerns a double movement, upwards and downwards, in the life of Christ. The mystery of Christ, he says, includes Jesus' worship, which he offers up as man, of his Father and the outpouring of the Holy Spirit at Pentecost, which he could only send down after his human nature had been glorified by his resurrection.[26] The greatest act of worship which Jesus offered to his Father was his obedience in dying on the Cross. In the double movement of his saving worship, Jesus *offers up* himself in a mystery of praise of his Father, and he thereby *brings down* the mystery of salvation for us.[27] The Catechism describes a similar movement, upwards and downwards, in its section on the worship offered by the

23. Ibid., p.71.
24. *The Mysteries of Christianity*, p.519.
25. J. Ratzinger, *Introduction to Christianity*, pp.239f.
26. Op. cit., p.197.
27. Ibid., 20.

Church in the liturgy of the sacraments: we offer worship to God, and God gives gifts that sanctify us.[28] Christ can do both, because he is God and man in one person. It is especially as our High Priest that Christ offered, and continues to offer in the heavenly sanctuary, the mystery of the worship of his Father, which culminated in the sacrifice of himself out of loving obedience on the Cross. This twofold movement is part of the task of every priest, who has to offer *up* sacrifice and prayers for the people and to call *down* gifts from above (cf. Hebr 5:1).

We can share in the mysteries of Christ's life because, as Schillebeeckx remarks, the redeeming acts of Christ's Paschal mystery are historical, yet they are perennial.[29] They were realized in history, and so are past, but they are also 'the same yesterday, today and forever' (cf. Hebr 13:8). The same point is made in the Catechism: the Paschal mystery is an historical event but it does not pass away: 'the event of the Cross and Resurrection *abides* and draws everything to life'.[30] The reason why the Paschal mystery does not remain only in the past but can be made present in all times is that by his death Christ destroyed death, and by his rising he restored life. In modern times, the theory that the sacraments make present again for us the mysteries of Christ's life was put forward by Dom Odo Casel (1886-1948) of Maria Laach Abbey, who was one of the pioneers of the liturgical movement preceding the Second Vatican Council. Casel's theory, however, has

---

28. CCC 1148.
29. Op. cit., p.55.
30. CCC 1085.

now been abandoned in its original form for the simple reason that what is past is past. The one exception is the Eucharist, in which the same sacrifice is offered as Christ offered on the Cross, although it is offered in another, unbloody way.

The correct solution to the difficulties found in Odo Casel's theory is put forward by Colman O'Neill, who says that the sacraments do not make the past mysteries themselves present, but their *effects*.[31] He points out that the sacraments signify what they effect: they effect what the various mysteries of Christ brought about for us. O'Neill reminds us that the past mysteries of Christ do not cause grace by themselves, but Christ's humanity, which has been shaped by those mysteries, causes grace, as his humanity 'full of grace and truth' is the source of grace for us. We now have contact with the humanity of Christ in the sacraments *as it has been affected* by the mysteries of his life: his Presentation, Baptism, Transfiguration and so on.[32] As O'Neill says, the sacraments 'reproduce' the mysteries of Christ in us.[33] For example, baptism associates us with the death and resurrection of Christ: as Christ first had to suffer in order to enter into glory (Lk 24:26), so we have to die and rise again with Christ sacramentally in order to enter into heaven.[34] Christ's death and resurrection are the source of new life in us when we are incorporated into his body, which underwent death and resurrection. Thus the

---

31. *Meeting Christ in the Sacraments*, p.63.
32. Ibid., p.61.
33. Ibid., p.77.
34. E. Schillebeeckx, *Christ the Sacrament*, p.45.

Paschal mystery is the cause and model of our rebirth in the Spirit (spiritual regeneration): as Christ died for our sins, so *by dying with him in baptism*, we die to sin in order to rise to new life with him (Rom 6:3-4).

In Romans 6:3-11, St Paul speaks of our *spiritual* resurrection in this life as a result of dying and rising with Christ. In 1 Corinthians 15:35-56, he speaks of our *bodily* resurrection at the end of time, when our lowly body will be conformed with Christ's risen body (cf. Phil 3:21). The first leads to the second: 'A necessary preliminary to final conformation is configuration to the mysteries of Christ in the present life', O'Neill says.[35] Thus the mysteries of Christ are central to the life of the Church as they are 1) the pattern of conforming, and being conformed, with Christ, and 2) they are the source of life. St Paul calls the risen body of Christ 'a life-giving spirit' (1 Cor 15:45). This does not mean that Christ is only spirit or that his body is not risen, but his risen body is spiritual, compared with the natural body of the first Adam, into which God only breathed the breath of natural life (Gen 2:7). As Leo the Great said, 'Our resurrection has begun with Christ's.'[36]

In order to share in the mysteries of Christ's life, we first have to be incorporated into his body by baptism. This is why the Church is necessary for our salvation, because she is the mystical Body of Christ. As O'Neill says, the mysteries of Christ influence those who belong to his body.[37] His mysteries still influence us, because each

---

35. Op. cit., p.46.
36. *Sermo de Resurrectione* 1,4.
37. Op. cit., p.53.

mystery brings its own special grace for our salvation. For example, the mystery of the Transfiguration brings us the grace of being transformed gradually, 'from glory to glory', as St Paul says (2 Cor 3:18). Fr John Saward corroborates O'Neill's solution that the sacraments do not make the mysteries themselves present but their effects, when he says that the mysteries of Christ still influence us, not in their historical circumstances but in their spiritual fruits, which abide forever.[38] This is supported by Pius XII, who taught that the mysteries of Christ live on in their effects in us, since each one of them is the cause of our salvation.[39] The principal mystery is the Paschal mystery, which we recall every time that we celebrate Mass. The pattern of Christ's mysteries is impressed on us by the sacraments as we die and rise with Christ, first through baptism. Colman O'Neill says, 'To receive a sacrament is to enter into communion with acts which made the events of Christ's life saving mysteries'.[40] All Christ's mysteries are our mysteries, because he is the Head of his mystical Body, the Church: Head and members make one body.[41] Here again we see the importance of belonging to the Church for participating in the mysteries of Christ's life. The external rite of only two of the sacraments refers clearly to Christ's Passover of his death and resurrection: namely baptism and the Eucharist. As Christ returned to his Father by his Passover (cf. Jn 13:1), so our way of

---

38. *Cradle of Redeeming Love*, p.69.
39. *Mediator Dei*, no. 176
40. *Meeting Christ in the Sacraments*, p.76
41. J. Saward, op. cit., p.66, quoting Columba Marmion, *Christ in his Mysteries*, p.25.

returning from this world to the Father lies in our being associated with these mysteries in a sacramental way. The only way to follow Christ, O'Neill says, is to pass through the mysteries of Christ's death and resurrection, which we do sacramentally in baptism.[42] Baptism is meant to be matched by a new life of conversion. In the Eucharist, we recall Christ's passion and death (his crossing over to the Father) and share in his risen life by receiving his body that has been raised up from the dead to life again.

The mysteries of Christ are, each in their own way, sources of grace and examples of perfection for us. Thus receiving the sacraments requires us to correspond with them by leading a life which reflects Christ's example. His mysteries are sources of grace because he is God, and examples of perfection because he is also man. As St Leo the Great pointed out, if Christ were not God, he could not supply the remedy; if he were not man, he would not supply an example, which it is possible for us to imitate.[43] We can imitate Christ because he is a man like us, except for sin. To give an example, Christ's Passion is an example of the virtues of patience, humility and self-denial, and of all the virtues we need for being saved.

As we have already noted, grace is caused by the glorified humanity of Christ as it has been shaped by the mysteries of his life. The mysteries of his life, death and resurrection were his way to glory, and sharing in them through the sacraments is our way to the life of glory in heaven. There is no other way for us than the way of Christ, who

---

42. Op. cit., p.45.
43. *In nativitate Domini sermo* 10, 2.

passed through his Passion, death and resurrection to his exaltation in glory. The mysteries of his life on earth are the foundation of his life in heaven, where he is seated at the right hand of the Father and, as our High Priest, continues to act in the sacraments through the power of his Holy Spirit. According to the Catechism, the Holy Spirit makes present the mystery of Christ in the liturgy: 'By his transforming power; he (the Holy Spirit) makes the mystery of Christ present here and now'.[44]

---

44. CCC 1092.

Chapter Three
Christis the Sacrament

The first sacrament is Christ himself, who is the source of all the sacraments as all grace comes through his humanity. We can speak of 'Christ the sacrament', because grace comes to us in a visible form in the sacraments and, as St Paul says, the grace of God appeared visibly in Jesus Christ when he became man (Tit 2:11; 3:5). The incarnate Son is also the sacrament of God, because he is the Image of God who is invisible (Col 1:15). As Jesus said to Philip, 'Whoever has seen me has seen the Father' (Jn 14:9). We can, then, say that the first sacrament is the incarnation, when God became visible in Jesus.

Christ is also the first sacrament because his humanity is the instrument of his divinity, just as the sacraments are instrumental causes of grace (they are the means which God uses to cause grace in us). Christ's humanity was an instrument of his divinity, because he acted in a divine way through his humanity. For example, he healed people as God by touching them as man (Mt 9:29). All Christ's saving activity was sacramental, because he was God acting in a human way through his body, to heal and save men and women. Jesus' redeeming acts are the sign and cause of grace, just as the sacraments are signs and causes of grace (how the sacraments cause grace will be discussed fully later in chapter seven).[45]

---

45. Cf. E. Schillebeeckx, *Christ the Sacrament*, p.16.

In Schillebeeckx's view, when Christ passed from our sight at his ascension, the sacraments came into operation as the means by which Christ continues to act in us and we can encounter Christ in his glorified humanity. There was no need for sacraments before Christ ascended; because men and women could meet him in his bodily presence, as we meet one another. Now we meet Christ through the bodily signs of the sacraments, as explained earlier in this chapter. A sign of this is that the Apostles were not baptised, except as the Holy Spirit was poured out on them at Pentecost, but St Paul, who did not know Christ in his earthly life, was baptised (Acts 9:18).

It is now common to speak also of the Church as a sacrament. Père Henri de Lubac expresses this clearly when he writes that the Church is the sacrament of Christ, as Christ is the sacrament of God.[46] The Church is the 'fundamental' sacrament, because she is the mystical Body of Christ and the fullness of Christ's Body. This is well explained by Matthias Scheeben who, writing in the middle of the nineteenth century, said that the Church is a sacrament as she is the mystical Body of Christ.[47] Scheeben remarks that in every sacrament, something is hidden and something is visible.[48] Thus the incarnation was a sacrament, because Christ's divinity was hidden in his visible flesh. As the mystery of the union of human nature with the divine Word was hidden in Christ's flesh, so, in the thought of Scheeben, Christ's flesh was raised to a mystery in the Eucharist, as it is made

---

46. *The Splendour of the Church*, p.147.
47. *The Mysteries of Christianity*, p.581.
48. Ibid., p.560.

present though hidden, beneath the visible appearances of bread and wine. Scheeben says that the Church becomes a sacrament by its connection with the incarnation and the Eucharist.[49] The mystery hidden in the visible Church is her union with Christ as his mystical Body, and with the Holy Spirit. Scheeben says that the Son of God could only acquire a mystical body by first assuming a body (Scheeben says 'entering' a body but 'assuming' is better).[50] It follows from the thought of Scheeben that the Church is a sacrament because Christ, by his incarnation, is first a sacrament and indeed that the sacrament of the Church continues the sacrament of the incarnation.

She is a sacrament, because she is a visible body on earth, although united in one Church with the blessed in heaven and the souls of those who still have to complete their way in Purgatory. The Church is called a sacrament in the opening paragraph of *Lumen Gentium*, the Second Vatican Council's charter of the Church: 'the Church, in Christ, is a sacrament – a sign and instrument, that is, of communion with God and of the unity of the entire human race'. The Church is a sacrament, because she is the visible sign of salvation in the world.[51] This does not mean, however, that only those visibly in the Church can be saved, but that salvation comes to the world through the Church. As Schillebeeckx says, the Church is a sacrament because she is 'the visible presence of grace'.[52] She is a sacrament, because all the sacraments are actions of the Church as well as of Christ.

---

49. Ibid., p.561.
50. Ibid., p.565.
51. SC 1, 5.
52. Op cit., p.7.

In Henri de Lubac's view, the unique mission of the Church is to make Christ present to men.[53] The Second Vatican Council taught that Christ is present in four ways: in his priest, above all in the Eucharist, in the word of God as it is proclaimed in the Church, and in the community of the faithful gathered in prayer.[54] 'Where two or three are gathered together in my name, there am I in the midst of them' (Matt 18:20). The same Vatican Council said that Christ is especially present in the Church in her liturgical actions.[55] Christ communicates his work of salvation to us through the liturgy of the Church, which is his action.[56] Fr Herbert Vorgrimler has described the Church as a sacrament, as she is the community of disciples filled with, and guided by, the Holy Spirit.[57]

We cannot have the Holy Spirit without the Son, for he sends the Holy Spirit; and we cannot have the Son without the Church, for she is his mystical body. The way we are incorporated into Christ is by being incorporated into his Body, the Church. Nor, as Père de Lubac points out, can we have the Holy Spirit without the Church; we cannot have the Spirit of Christ without his Body, the Church, just as body and spirit belong together in human nature and make a unity. De Lubac's point comes from St Irenaeus (martyred c. 200), who wrote: 'To sever yourself from the Church is to reject the Spirit'.[58] Augustine made

53. *The Splendour of the Church*, p.161.
54. SC 7.
55. Ibid., 7.
56. CCC 1076.
57. *Sacramental Theology*, pp.32f.
58. *Adversus Haereses* 3 c.24, 1.

a similar point: 'To live by the Spirit of Christ, one must remain in his body'.[59] God communicates his grace to us through the Church, because all grace comes through the humanity of Christ and the Church is his mystical Body.

This gives us a threefold distinction of sacrament:

1. Christ is the first sacrament.
2. The Church is the fundamental sacrament.
3. The seven sacraments (baptism, confirmation etc.).

The seven sacraments come from, and actualise, the sacrament of the Church, because they are actions of the Church. The Church is a sacrament, because she is the mystical Body of Christ and the visible sign of grace and salvation in the world. She has an outward, visible structure, which is commonly seen in her three functions of witness (*marturia*), of liturgy (*leitourgia*), and of service (*diakonia*). Thus the Church, which includes all the faithful, is visible to the world in her preaching of the Gospel (witness), in her prayer centred around the sacraments (liturgy), and in her service of the poor. She is especially visible in her celebration of the sacraments. St Thomas Aquinas, echoing a thought of the Fathers of the Church, says that the Church was fashioned (*fabricata*) out of the sacraments which flowed from the side of Christ on the Cross when water and blood, symbolising baptism and the Eucharist, flowed from his side.[60] The Catechism too speaks of 'the wondrous sacrament of the Church', which was born from Christ's side on the Cross.[61]

---

59. *Sermon* 267, 4; 268, 2.
60. ST 3a 64, 2 ad 3.
61. CCC 1067, quoting SC 5.

Chapter Four

Christ's Worship of the Father

For St Thomas Aquinas, all the sacraments have a double function: they free us from sin and perfect us for the worship of God.[62] These two functions are connected by the cross, for Christ's sacrifice on the cross, by which he liberated us from sin, was also his act of perfect worship of the Father. They free us from sin because they are all connected with the Passion of Christ, by which he freed us from sin. The worship we offer to God in the liturgy of the Church is a participation in the worship which the Son offered as man to his Father. In order to offer this worship, he took a human nature like ours, except for sin (Hebr 10:5-10). Taking up St Thomas' thought, Schillebeeckx describes the sacraments as 'the visible realisation on earth of Christ's saving mystery of worship'.[63] As we have already noted, Schillebeeckx sees a double movement in the worship, which Christ offered to his Father: a mystery of praise which he offers upwards, and the mystery of salvation, which he brings down. The first he offers up as man, supremely on the Cross; the second he brings down as God through his humanity, in which he offers his worship as man. Christ took up his body and blood, which he sacrificed on the cross, to present them to his

62. ST 3a 62, 5; 65, 1.
63. *Christ the Sacrament*, p.53.

Father as a living and eternal sacrifice, by his resurrection and ascension. Durrwell remarks that there is a liturgy, or worship, in heaven, but there is no worship unless Christ has a sacrifice to offer in the heavenly sanctuary.[64]

Christ continues to offer worship to his Father in the heavenly sanctuary as our great High Priest: there he lives for ever to intercede for us (Hebr 7:25). Colman O'Neill explains that the heart of Christ's sacrifice was his obedience to the will of his Father. This is brought out by the writer of the Letter to the Hebrews, who puts into the mouth of Christ the words of the Psalmist: 'Here I am; I have come to do your will' (Hebr 10:5-7; Ps 39:6-8). The Psalmist is making the point that God does not want burnt offerings but obedience, which is sacrifice of will. Christ expressed his obedience, which is an interior act of worship, in the mysteries of his life, and his attitude of obedience by which he lived on earth still remains eternally in heaven, just as the virtues we possess in this life shape us for eternity.[65] It is in this sense that we can say that Christ's sacrifice lasts forever in heaven. His sacrifice is eternal, because the acts of Christ's mind, with which he offered, namely his charity and obedience, remain forever in his human mind.[66] The sacrifice is also eternal because it is once-for-all (Hebr 10:12).

The sacraments are the means by which Christ brings down salvation to us now as they are actions of the Church, which Christ uses to achieve his work of salvation, for he instituted the sacraments. They are actions of the Church,

---

64. *The Resurrection*, p.143. Cf. Hebr 8:3.
65. *Meeting Christ in the Sacraments*, p.7.
66. Ibid., p.57.

the mystical Body of Christ, in which he acts. As already noted, Christ is present in his minister, in the Eucharist, in the proclamation of the word of God, which is a part of all the sacraments, and in the praying community. Schillebeeckx says that a sacrament is both a personal act of Christ, realized in visible form, and a visible action of the Church as the institution of redemption. As the Catechism says, Christ is always present in his Church to communicate the work of salvation.[67] Christ acts through the Church, because she is his body. And he acts in the sacraments, because it is Christ himself who baptises, forgives sin, speaks the words of consecration, offers the sacrifice of himself in the Mass.[68]

The liturgy has two poles: on the side of the Church, it is an act of faith; on the side of Christ, he enters the liturgy to act in it. Christ acts now in and through his body, the Church, just as he once did on earth, when people saw him, touched him and met him with bodily presence. But the sacraments do not exist except as signs of the Church's faith, for they are only performed within the context of people sharing the faith of the Church.[69] The sacraments are his acts realised as acts of the Church.[70] They constitute the mystery of the worship of Christ as it can be seen in the Church.[71] The mysteries of Christ's life are all part of his worship as they led up to his sacrifice

---

67. CCC 1088.
68. Pius XII, *Mystici Corporis* (1943), AAS vol. 35, p.218.
69. C. O'Neill, op. cit., p.71.
70. E. Schillebeeckx, op. cit., p.59; cf. p.66.
71. Ibid., p.70.

on the Cross: for example, his Presentation in the Temple and his Baptism clearly point to his death on the Cross. These mysteries last for ever, because Christ's entire life on earth was a living out, in a human way, of his eternal relationship to the Father as the Son.[72] The mysteries of Christ's life, as St Leo the Great said, have now passed over into the sacraments. The liturgy of every sacrament includes a reference to the saving events of Christ's life in the readings from Scripture or in its prayers.

Every sacrament has a past, present and future significance.[73] In its past significance, it commemorates a past event: for example, the Eucharist commemorates the Passion of Christ. This past significance is also *anamnesis* which, in its biblical meaning, is the recalling of a past event in a way that also makes it present or actual today.[74] In its present significance, the sacrament bestows grace and communicates an effect of the Passion: for example, the forgiveness of sin in confession or Christ's love for his Bride, the Church, shown on the Cross, in marriage. In its future reference, a sacrament is a pledge of salvation and leads us to future glory in heaven. Explaining this teaching in a contemporary way, Colman O'Neill says that the sacraments signify (are signs of) our sanctification in a threefold way. They signify the Passion of Christ in the past; they signify grace as a present reality; and they signify the eternal life which is to come. The central one of these three meanings for O'Neill is the second one, the present reality, rather than the historical mysteries. The

---

72. Ibid., p.58.
73. ST 3a 60, 3.
74. For a useful explanation of *anamnesis*, see John Paul II, *Rosarium Virginis Mariae*, 13.

past and future meanings are subordinate to the present one: the past meaning is directed to it, the future one flows from it.[75]

We have said that the sacraments are acts of Christ and acts of the Church, because she is the mystical Body of Christ. Thus the worship of the Church, offered in the liturgy of the sacraments, prolongs on earth the priesthood of Christ, which he now exercises in the heavenly sanctuary.[76] Colman O'Neill says that the sacramental system of the Church is centred around the heavenly worship of Christ.[77] The sacraments are the worship of the *whole* Church, of her Head and members together. As the Catechism says:

> Liturgy is an 'action' of the whole Christ (*totus Christus*). Those who even now celebrate it without signs are already in the heavenly liturgy.[78]

The liturgy in heaven consists of the adoration of the Lamb, who stands on the throne 'as though slain' (Rev 5:8).

> It is in this eternal liturgy that the Spirit and the Church enable us to participate whenever we celebrate the mystery of salvation in the sacraments.[79]

Thus the liturgy of the Church on earth participates in the heavenly liturgy of the adoration of the Lamb, which

---

75. Op. cit., pp.68f.
76. E. Schillebeeckx, *Christ the Sacrament*, p.197.
77. Op. cit., p.40.
78. CCC 1136.
79. CCC 1139.

shows that the sacrifice Christ offered as our High Priest goes on for ever in the heavenly sanctuary, because he is the Lamb who still appears 'as though slain'. Jesus came on earth, to lead us into the heavenly sanctuary. The way he entered it was through the sacrifice of his obedience and suffering. Just as the high priests in the Old Testament entered the Holy of Holies once a year to offer the sacrifice of atonement, so Christ has opened up for us 'the new and living way' through the veil of his flesh (Hebr 10:20). Christ entered the Holy of Holies by his bodily ascension, and our way into the heavenly sanctuary lies in the sacraments which, as we have seen, give us a share in the worship which Christ offers as our High Priest to the Father in the Holy Spirit (cf. Hebr 9:14). As the liturgy is an action of Christ and of the Church together, we next go on to say more about how Christ acts in the sacraments.

Chapter Five
Acts of Christ

Christ continues to act in the sacraments, because he instituted them. The question whether Christ instituted all seven of the sacraments of the Catholic Church has been much disputed since the Middle Ages until today. At the Reformation in the sixteenth century, many Protestants only accepted two sacraments, baptism and the Eucharist, because they held that only these two are explicitly mentioned in the New Testament. Among Catholic writers today, Michael Lawler thinks that Christ instituted some of the sacraments only implicitly, merely by founding the Church.[80] This idea is found in Fr Karl Rahner.[81] Lawler, for example, denies that Christ instituted confirmation.[82] St Thomas Aquinas thought that Christ instituted confirmation by promising to send the Holy Spirit. He sent the Holy Spirit when he breathed on the Apostles on the day of his resurrection and at Pentecost.

It seems to me, however, that something more is meant by the institution of the sacraments by Christ than Lawler admits. When we look closely at the New Testament, we find fairly definite mention of penance (Matt 16:19; 18:18; Jn 20:23), anointing of the sick (Mk 6:13; Jam 5:14), and

---

80. *Sacrament and Symbol*, pp.49f.
81. *The Church and the Sacraments*, p.41.
82. Op. cit., p.50.

ordination (Lk 22:19; Hebr 7:24). Christ himself was a priest – the High Priest of the New Covenant, which lasts for ever. We can infer that marriage is a sacrament, because St Paul calls it 'a great mystery' (Eph 5:32). '*Musterion*' was the Greek word for a sacrament in the early Church. With regard to confirmation, the Holy Spirit, whom Christ promised to send, came down on the Apostles visibly at Pentecost. Thus there is good evidence for all seven sacraments in the New Testament itself.

Schillebeeckx holds that Christ only established the 'sevenfold direction' of the sacraments, but left the determination of their outward sign to the Church.[83] It should be said, however, that the meaning and direction of a sacrament go intrinsically with the essential sign and the 'form' of words of a sacrament: what the sacrament is for, is indicated by the essential words, the 'form' of the sacrament. We shall see how much the Church or a Pope can lay down what constitutes the essential rite of a sacrament when we come to the individual sacraments of confirmation and ordination. Pius XII held that the Church has no power to change the 'substance' of any of the sacraments.[84] The 'substance' of a sacrament is usually understood to mean whatever Christ determined about it, as far as we know from the sources of revelation. We can see that Christ meant there to be a sacrament of penance but he may not have determined the precise words or form of the sacrament. Bernard Leeming S.J. says that Christ at least instituted the seven sacraments by settling the meaning of the sign of each sacrament, as it is by giving a

83. *Christ the Sacrament*, pp.140f.
84. *Constitution on Orders* (1948), n.1.

sign a particular meaning which constitutes a sacrament.[85]

Christ instituted what is necessary for each sacrament: they all go back 'to the familiar tradition of the Apostles, although they have not all been handed down (*tradita*) in Scripture'.[86] The Council of Trent determined that the essential sign cannot be changed.[87] Lawler agrees that the Church cannot change the basic meaning, or purpose, of the sacraments, because they were instituted by Christ.[88] Aquinas gives as the reason why it is not in our power to determine what is essential to each sacrament, that God alone has the power to sanctify; so the sacraments have been divinely instituted.[89]

Since God alone is the source of grace and the sacraments have been instituted by his Son, the sacraments work '*ex opere operato*'. This phrase means that a valid sacrament takes place just by 'the work having been worked'. The 'work', in this case, is the sacrament. The phrase is contrasted with '*ex opere operantis*', 'by the work of the one who works it.' The former phrase means that a sacrament does not depend on the minister who performs it, for its effectiveness. The point of the phrase '*ex opere operato*' is, first of all, that the grace of the sacrament does not depend on the holiness of the minister, and, therefore, Christ is free, not limited by any lack of holiness in his minister. The sacraments are independent of the personal faith of the minister, although he must intend to do what the Church wills, since a sacrament always expresses the faith of the Church. If a

---

85. *The Principles of Sacramental Theology,* p.417.
86. Aquinas, ST 3a 64, 2 ad 1.
87. Session 7, canon 1. ND 1311.
88. Cf. ND 1311, 1324.
89. ST 3a 60, 5.

sacrament depended on the grace and faith of the minister, it would only work *ex opere operantis*. It was St Augustine who established, as a result of the Donatist controversy in northern Africa, that the sacraments work *ex opere operato*. The Donatists, named after their leader, Donatus, formed a schismatic church because they refused to accept Caecilian as Bishop of Carthage in 311, as he had been consecrated by a bishop who they claimed had apostatised. Thus they held that the efficacy of the sacraments depended on the minister. Augustine established once for all that the validity of a sacrament does not depend on the personal state of the minister but on its being an action of the Church. The grace it confers is not more or less as it is performed by a more or less worthy priest, although the good example of a priest may have an added influence on those to whom he ministers.

The sacraments work *ex opere operato* because they do not derive their power from the minister but from God, who is the sole cause of grace. They are effective signs: that is, they cause grace by signifying it and they effect the grace which they signify. In the words of the prophet Isaiah, like the word of God, they accomplish what they were sent to do (Isa 55:11). Since they bestow *sanctifying* grace, they also increase charity in the recipient, and so produce in us, St Thomas Aquinas says, a likeness of the Holy Spirit, who is the Love of the Father and the Son.[90] Sanctifying grace, which transforms us and produces habitual grace, is distinguished from actual grace, which is the grace God gives us for every single good action as each occasion requires. We still need actual grace for every good choice and decision even when we are in a state of habitual grace.

---

90. ST 2a 2ae 24, 5 ad 3.

The faith of the recipient of a sacrament is not a cause of grace but a necessary *disposition* for receiving grace.

Schillebeeckx lists four conditions, which are necessary for a sacrament to be a saving act of Christ, in other words, for it to be effective in the recipient.

1. *The Church's word of faith.* This is the essential words, which constitute the 'form' of a sacrament. (The form of a thing is what makes its matter be the kind of thing it is.)

2. *The intention of the minister.* He must intend to do what the Church intends, because a sacrament is an act of the Church. The minister does not have to be holy, or even have faith, but he has to perform it with the intention of the Church and, for most sacraments, be a validly ordained priest of the Church (in apostolic succession).

3. *The intention of the recipient.* Except in the case of the Eucharist, when the sacrament of Christ's Body and Blood already exists after the consecration before it is received by anyone, a sacrament is not effective unless the recipient receives it with a suitable disposition.

All the sacraments, except the Eucharist, are null and void without the faith of the recipient. It is impossible to be baptised without assenting to the Faith of the Church, because baptism is the sacrament of faith. In the case of infants, who cannot yet have knowledge of this faith or express assent to it, the faith of their parents or godparents stands in place of faith for them. There is a giving and receiving in the sacraments: they do not work automatically. A gift is not given unless it is also received. The recipient must respond willingly.[91] But grace is given infallibly to those who are suitably disposed, because a

91. C. O'Neill, op. cit., pp.133f.

sacrament works *ex opere operato*.

4. *The sacrament was instituted by Christ*. The essential sign cannot be changed: for example, bread and wine must be used in the Eucharist and there must be a washing with water in baptism. This point has already been discussed above at the beginning of this section.

Michael Lawler points out that St Thomas Aquinas does not use the phrase '*ex opere operato*' in his later *Summa Theologiae* but only in his earlier commentary *On the Sentences IV*. Lawler holds that the phrase, as used by St Thomas, refers to the efficacy of Christ's Passion in the sacraments.[92] He observes that the two phrases '*ex opere operato*' and '*ex opere operantis*' were not contrasted, or opposed, in the Scholastic theologians of the thirteenth century, but went together. No sacrament mediates grace without the recipient playing a part, but a sacrament is constituted objectively just by being performed. No sacrament is fruitful without the *opus operantis*, which consists in the conversion and charity of the recipient. Both parties, a minister of the Church and the recipient, are required, for a 'personal encounter' with Christ to take place in a sacrament. The sacraments are signs of the faith of the Church and of the recipient, as well as of the recipient's desire to be saved.[93] The Council of Florence (1439) said that 'the sacraments give grace to those who receive them worthily', and the Council of Trent 'to those who place no obstacle' in the way of grace.[94] We next consider the grace which each sacrament gives.

---

92. Op. cit., p.38.
93. M. Lawler, op. cit., p.40.
94. DS 1310, 1606.

Chapter Six
Signs of Grace

Having seen how the sacraments are founded on the mysteries of Christ's life and give us a participation in the worship which Christ offers to his Father as our High Priest, we now consider what the sacraments are in themselves and what they do to us. In the early Church, the Greek word for the sacraments was *musteria*, the 'mysteries'. The word *musterion* does not mean a sacrament in the New Testament but, as used by St Paul, God's hidden plan of salvation, which has now been revealed (Eph 3:4). The word comes from *muein*, to cover up, and so suggests something hidden. In the early Church, the sacraments were only openly explained to those who had been initiated into the Church: they were kept hidden from those outside her. *Musterion* was first used for a sacrament by Clement of Alexandria and Origen in the early third century. Clement of Alexandria meant by '*musterion*' 'a representation of sacred things through perceptible signs'.[95]

In the Western Church, the word '*sacramentum*' was first used for baptism and the Eucharist by Tertullian (c.160-225).[96] In secular use, this word meant the oath of faithful service, which a soldier made to the leader of his regiment.

---

95. M. Lawler, *Sacrament and Symbol*, p.30.
96. Lawler cites *De Baptismo* 1 (PL vol 1, 1197) and *De Corona* 11 (PL 2, 91).

It was transferred to the sacraments of the Christians as a Christian is someone dedicated to the service of Christ. As a soldier in the Roman army was marked with a sign of the legion to which he belonged, so the sacraments which confer 'character' (this will be discussed later) imprint, as it were, on us God's mark of ownership and sign us for the service and worship of Christ.

The next development of the meaning of sacrament, in the West, came from St Augustine, who was the first to call sacraments 'signs'.[97] Augustine distinguishes between the sign, which is seen, and what it signifies, which is believed. The reality which is signified, for example, the forgiveness of sins or union with Christ or a sacred 'character', is effected by Christ and the Holy Spirit. Thus a sacrament is an *efficacious* sign. This distinguishes the sacraments from other signs and symbols.[98] The difference between a sign and a sacrament, then, is that a sign only signifies but a sacrament also effects, or brings about what it signifies. Thus a sacrament is a *cause* of grace, as we shall see in the next section. Augustine is important for showing that a sacrament consists of a sign and a reality. The reality is the grace it signifies. This also will be explained more fully below when we come to the mystery of grace and the mystery of the Church.

For Peter Lombard (c.1100-1150), who wrote the *Sentences* which became the standard text book for the scholastic theologians, like St Thomas and St Bonaventure, to comment on, a sacrament is a cause of grace.

---

97. *Civitas Dei* X, c.5.
98. M. Lawler, op. cit., p.32.

> A sacrament, properly speaking, is a sign of the grace of God and the form of invisible grace in such a way that it is its image and cause.[99]

For St Thomas Aquinas, who develops Augustine's idea of a sign, a sacrament is first of all a *sacred sign*.[100] It is a sign of a sacred reality as it sanctifies us.[101] Aquinas says that it is natural for us to begin with things which we perceive with the senses (called 'sensibles'), in order to come to knowledge of things which we can only grasp with the mind (intelligibles). A sign is that by which we come to the knowledge of something else. Thus a heart is a sign of love, a peacock of immortality, and so on. A sacrament is a sign which signifies the reality of what God does in us through it, and it also sanctifies us. Indeed, these two go together: we are sanctified in receiving the reality, which the sign signifies. This reality, as we shall explain more fully below, is the effect of interior grace, which God works in us through the sacrament. Thus the sacraments are sacred signs, because they sanctify us.

We have seen how Peter Lombard already spoke of the 'form' of a sacrament. For Lombard, this was the invisible grace. But for Aquinas the form was the essential words of a sacrament: for example, the words of consecration for the Eucharist, 'I baptise you' in the threefold name of the Trinity in baptism, 'I absolve you from your sins etc.' for penance. As a sacrament has its form, so it has its matter: matter and form go together to constitute a

---

99. *Liber Sententiarum* IV d.1 c.4.
100. ST 3a 60, 1.
101. ST 3a 60, 2.

sacrament, just as St Augustine had said, 'A word comes to an element and a sacrament is made'.[102] For Augustine, the element was the material sign used in the sacrament, like water, bread or oil. But not all the sacraments use some material; so the matter of some sacraments is an action, like confessing one's sins or exchanging promises (in marriage). As the form of a thing makes it be the kind of thing it is, so the form of the words determines what the matter of the sacrament is a sign of. For example, the essential words of baptism, 'I baptise you in the name of the Father etc.' make the pouring of water into a spiritual cleansing.[103] The words and actions of a sacrament are inseparable.

The tradition, which St Thomas sums up for us on this point, is reflected in the new *Catechism of the Catholic Church*, which calls sacraments 'perceptible signs', consisting of words and actions.[104] The sacraments are 'powers', which come forth from the body of Christ and actions of the Holy Spirit at work in the Church.[105] Power went out of Christ's body when he was touched by those seeking to be healed by him (Lk 8:46). We find a good definition of a sacrament in the Catechism 1131: a sacrament is an efficacious sign of grace, instituted by Christ, by which divine life is communicated to us. The visible rites of the sacraments signify and make present the grace proper to each sacrament. They bear fruit (through

---

102. *In Ev. Ioannis Tract.* 80, 3.
103. ST 3a 60, 6.
104. CCC 1084.
105. CCC 1116.

giving grace) in those who receive them with the right disposition, that is with faith and in a state of grace and charity. The sacraments are effective signs because, as St Paul remarks, God's word is a word of *power*: 'for our Gospel came to you not only in word, but also in power and in the Holy Spirit' (1 Thess 1:5). Our next step, then, is to consider in more detail how the sacraments cause grace.

Chapter Seven
Causes of Grace

In the previous section, we saw that the sacraments are a special kind of sign: they cause the reality which they signify. As St Thomas Aquinas says, the sacraments both signify grace and cause it.[106] They are signs and causes: they bring about what they signify. Colman O'Neill specifies that the sacraments cause grace by signifying it but, properly speaking, they do not cause as signs, for God and Christ are the efficient causes of grace, who use the signs of the sacraments.[107] Signs are distinct from causes; a sign by itself produces knowledge in us, but the sacraments also cause grace. In this, the sacraments of the New Testament differ from those of the Old Testament. The sacraments of the Old Testament were only signs as the sacrifices of the Old Testament prefigured the Passion of Christ, but they did not cause grace. The Old Testament had sacraments, because it was necessary for the coming of the Christ to be foretold by signs.[108] Just as no one can be saved except by the Passion of Christ, so people in the Old Testament could be saved by faith in Christ *as he was still to come*. They showed their faith in him by offering the sacrifices divinely prescribed in the ritual of the Old

---

106. ST 62, 1 ad 3; 62, 3.
107. Loc. cit., p.70.
108. ST 3a 61, 3.

Testament. These sacrifices prefigured the sacrifice of Christ on the cross, which was all three kinds of sacrifice in the Old Testament in one: expiation, peace offering and holocaust. Thus the sacraments of the Old Testament were demonstrations of faith but they could not cause grace, because Christ had not yet died on the Cross. Baptism is prefigured in the Old Testament by circumcision, the Eucharist by the Passover, and ordination by the anointing of priests. As Schillebeeckx remarks, the grace of Christ is already foreshadowed in the history of Israel, for the Church is the continuation of Israel.

The principal cause of grace in the sacraments is *God*, for all grace comes from God. The sacraments are *instrumental* causes, which God uses to communicate the saving power and life that the mysteries of Christ's life, death and resurrection, gained for us. The sacraments get their power from being divinely instituted by Christ, who is God as well as man.[109] St Thomas says that the sacraments work like instruments: instruments depend on being moved by an agent for producing an effect.[110] For example, a pen is an instrument of writing, but it does not write any words unless it is moved by the hand of a writer. The letters produced with a pen depend more on the writer than on the pen. There are two kinds of instruments: one is *joined* to the agent, the other is *separate* from the agent. Taking over the idea of St John Damascene (d. 749), that Christ's humanity is an instrument of his divinity, Aquinas

---

109. ST 3a 64, 3.
110. ST 3a 62, 1; 62, 4.

says that the humanity of Christ is a joined instrument, but the sacraments are separate instruments. A hand is a joined instrument of the body, but a chisel is a separate instrument of a carpenter. Fr John Saward says that grace passes from the Triune God into the sacraments through the humanity of Christ.[111]

Thus Christ causes grace *as God and as man*, but in different ways. As he is God, he causes grace 'authoritatively', for God is the Author and principal cause of grace. As he is man, Christ's power is as the principal minister, for he is our High Priest as man. As man, Christ is the cause of grace in several ways. First, he causes grace *meritoriously*, since he merited by his charity and by humbling himself, so that he was exalted. He causes grace *instrumentally*, since grace comes through his humanity, which is a joined instrument of his divinity. And he causes grace *efficiently*, as he healed people by his human actions, although with divine power.[112] Christ cannot communicate his power of authority as the Author of grace to men, but he can communicate his 'power of excellence', which he possesses as our great High Priest.[113] Since he can communicate his power of excellence, he can act through the ministry of his priests.

The sacraments are causes of grace, then, because Christ works in them.[114] They do not obtain their effect so much by the prayer of the Church as by the merits of Christ's Passion. As St Leo the Great says, the Cross is the source

---

111. *Cradle of Redeeming Love*, p.97.
112. ST 3a 64, 3.
113. ST 3a 64, 4.
114. C. O'Neill, op. cit., p.78.

of every grace and blessing.[115] As we have already noted, according to St Thomas Aquinas, the sacraments have a double purpose: to be a remedy for sin and to perfect us for the worship of God.[116] They derive their power for both these purposes from the Passion of Christ. Echoing the tradition of the Fathers of the Church, St Thomas saw the sign of this in the water and blood which flowed from Christ's side on the Cross (Jn 19:34). The water and blood symbolised the sacraments, first of all, baptism and the Eucharist. The sacraments perfect us for sharing in the worship of Christ, because the liturgy of the Church is a participation in the perfect worship offered by Christ as our eternal High Priest to his Father in the heavenly sanctuary. This is especially true in the offering of the sacrifice of the Mass. The sacraments are signs of grace, Colman O'Neill says, because they recreate in liturgical action the saving actions of Christ in his humanity.[117] All his saving actions led up to the Cross, from which the grace of the sacraments flows. Colman O'Neill notes that, properly speaking, the sacraments do not cause grace but Christ's humanity is the instrumental cause of grace as it was affected by the mysteries of his life, death and resurrection.[118]

The sacraments are caused by the whole Paschal mystery: not just by the Passion of Christ but also by his resurrection. They are caused by his Passion as the starting point (*terminus a quo*), and by his resurrection

---

115. *Sermo de Passione* 8, 7.
116. ST 3a 61, 1.
117. Op. cit., p.78.
118. Ibid., p.61.

as the end (*terminus ad quem*). The starting-point is the removal of sin; the end is new life. Christ gained the first by his Passion, and the second by his resurrection. St Paul saw that we are not only justified by the Passion of Christ but also by his resurrection: 'Jesus the Lord, who was put to death for our sins and raised for our justification' (Rom 4:25). Justification has two sides in the Catholic view: it is not just the forgiveness of sin, which in itself is just the removal of something, but also the gift of new life. Positively, justification works the interior renewal of the person. This comes from the new life which Christ brought us by his resurrection. We can never think of the grace of Christ apart from the mysteries of his life.

St Thomas thought that justification is an effect of all the sacraments.[119] Justification includes the forgiveness of sin, conversion of heart and the new life of transforming grace.[120] The Council of Trent affirmed, against the Protestant Reformers, that we are not justified by faith alone but that the sacraments also confer grace.[121] Writing as an Anglican in 1838, the Venerable John Henry Newman asserted against Lutherans that we are not justified by faith alone but also by baptism: in other words, by the sacraments. Newman asked whether justification just consisted in faith or also in renovation of the person. He came to the conclusion that neither of these two was sufficient, since justification above all 'consists in the coming and presence of the Holy Spirit

---

119. ST 3a 64, 1.
120. Cf. CCC 1987-1989 on justification.
121. Trent, session VII, canon 8 (ND 1318).

within us'.[122] 'This is really and truly our justification… the very presence of Christ'. 'Christ is our Righteousness by dwelling in us by the Spirit'.[123] The sacraments do not just mediate the presence of God to us, but renew and transform our human nature inwardly by grace.

Another effect of the sacraments is that they reproduce the likeness of Christ in us. As the way that Christ returned to his Father was by his death and resurrection, so we have to be conformed with him in his death and resurrection sacramentally, that is, by signs. This is done first of all by baptism, in which we are buried with Christ so that we may rise to new life (Rom 6:3-4). St Paul speaks of Christ being 'formed' in us (Gal 4:19). He is formed in us when we are conformed with him. We are 'predestined to be conformed to the image of the Son, so that he might be the first-born among many brethren' (Rom 8:29). The image of Christ is reproduced in us by the Holy Spirit, who conforms us to the image of Christ: 'and we all, with unveiled face, beholding the glory of the Lord, are being transformed into his image (*eikona*) from glory to glory; for this comes from the Lord who is the Spirit' (2 Cor 3:18). As we are transformed into the image of Christ by the Holy Spirit, the sacraments enable us to share in the effect of Christ's Transfiguration. Indeed the Catechism says that baptism is the sacrament of regeneration and the Transfiguration the sacrament of the second regeneration as it prefigures the resurrection of our body in glory.[124]

---

122. *Lectures on the Doctrine of Justification*, p.139; cf. pp.137, 144.
123. Ibid., p.150 cf; p.154.
124. CCC 556.

Chapter Eight

Mystery of Grace and Mystery of the Church

The sacraments, however, are not just a means of grace for the individual in isolation but they also deepen the recipient's relation to the Church as one of her members. The sacraments unite us with Christ in grace, because they put us in a relation with the Church.[125] As Schillebeeckx notes, the salvation of the individual is also ecclesial, that is, it is brought about in the Church, because we are reborn in the Church. We are fully incorporated into Christ by being incorporated into his mystical Body, the Church. Indeed, we cannot have the sacraments without the Church.

Thus every sacrament has three aspects: first, it has a sign. This is called the *sacramentum tantum*, the sacramental sign alone. Secondly, each sacrament relates us in a special way to the Church. This is called the reality and the sacrament (*res et sacramentum*). Thirdly, there is the reality alone (*res tantum* or, sometimes, *res sacramenti*, the reality of the sacrament). This is the effect of interior grace in the individual. St Thomas Aquinas says that the first, the sacrament alone, is the visible sign of the reality alone.[126] The late Fr Herbert McCabe O.P. rendered the second and third terms, the reality and the sacrament and the reality alone, respectively as the Mystery of the Church and the Mystery of grace, because every sacrament puts us in a

125. *Christ the Sacrament*, pp.218f.
126. ST 3a 66, 1.

special relation to the Church and produces an effect of interior grace in the individual.[127]

The sign alone (*sacramentum tantum*) of each sacrament is as follows. In baptism, it is washing with water; in the Eucharist, it is bread and wine; in confirmation, it is signing with chrism; in penance, the acts of the penitent (confession) and of the confessor (absolution); in anointing of the sick, it is anointing with oil; in ordination, it is the laying on of hands; in marriage, the words of consent or promises. The sign is not some material in every sacrament, like water, bread or oil, but can consist of actions, like confessing sins, the laying on of hands, or making and consenting to a promise. All these actions, however, are corporeal signs.

	Res et Sacramentum (Mystery of the Church)	Res tantum (Mystery of Grace)
Baptism	Character (share in priesthood of Christ)	Sanctifying grace, new life of the Spirit
Confirmation	Character	The fullness of the Holy Spirit, the seven Gifts
Eucharist	The Body and Blood of Christ	Charity, the Unity of the Church
Penance	Reconciliation with God through the Church	Conversion, interior repentance
Anointing	Restoration to the Church or Dying in Christ	Closer union with Christ
Ordination	Character (a permanent consecration)	Personal grace for the state and ministry of ordained person
Marriage	Union of the spouses , a permanent bond, as a sign of Christ's relation to the Church	Grace for the duties of married life

127. *The Teaching of the Catholic Church* (London, Catholic Truth Society 1985), p.15.

The reality and the sacrament (relation to the Church) and the reality alone (effect of interior grace), can best be seen in the chart above, where they are respectively labelled the mystery of the Church and the mystery of grace.

As every sacrament is an encounter with Christ in his Church, it is a mystery of the Church. For this reason every sacrament has a double effect; a relation to the Church and a relation to God and Christ. These are, respectively, the ecclesial effect and the effect of grace (the mystery of the Church and the mystery of grace). There is some dispute about what these two are in the case of some of the sacraments. For example, some today understandably hold that the unity of the Church is the Mystery of the Church in the Eucharist, and so ascribe the real Body and Blood of Christ to the mystery of grace. But Aquinas thought that the unity of the Church is a consequence of charity, and so was able to make the real Body and Blood of Christ be the reality and sacrament (*res et sacramentum*) of the Eucharist, which is the more traditional view. We see well how the two aspects, the mystery of the Church and of grace, are related in the case of penance: reconciliation with the Church (reality and sacrament) brings us the grace of interior conversion (reality alone).

Confirmation, in the view of Schillebeeckx, unites us with Christ as he is the Sender of the Holy Spirit.[128] Anointing of the sick incorporates us into the suffering

---

128. Op. cit., p.190.

Church and gives us victory over death. The sacrament of Orders makes the priest 'the sacramental Christ'.[129] He represents Christ bodily. Marriage is the sign of the relation of Christ to his Bride, the Church.

---

129. Ibid., p.212.

Chapter Nine
Character

The mystery of the Church, or *res et sacramentum*, of three of the seven sacraments is what we call 'character': they are baptism, confirmation and ordination. These are the three sacraments which cannot be repeated but only received once. They cannot be repeated for any individual, because they give an 'indelible' mark, which cannot be removed, even when the recipient totally lapses from grace or abandons his office. Once we become an adopted son or daughter of God, we can never loose this status, just as the so-called 'prodigal' son did not cease to be a son when he left his home but, when he returned, was treated by his father like a son as though he had never left (Lk 15:20-22). Once a man is ordained a priest, he is a priest for ever, because he shares in Christ's priesthood, which lasts for ever, as Christ lives for ever.[130] 'You are a priest for ever, according to the order of Melchisedek' (Ps 109:4; Hebr 7:17).

The word 'character' was originally the Greek for a letter carved or engraved in stone, or inscribed with ink. Hence it meant a letter, sign or symbol, impressed in some material surface, like stone or papyrus. The characters, or letters, we write are often revealing of our character, in the modern sense. For the purpose of the sacraments,

---

130. Cf. Heb 7:24.

character means a mark of ownership impressed in us, marking us for the service of Christ. It was common in the ancient world to mark soldiers with the sign of the leader or general, in whose legion they served.

The simplest way of explaining the 'character' conferred by sacraments is to say that it gives one *a participation in the priesthood of Christ*. Christ is the first person who has 'character', for he is said to be the very stamp (*'character'* in the original Greek text) of God's nature and the radiance of his glory (Hebr 1:3). Christ is the eternal 'character' of the Father's substance, for he is the image of God; sacramental character gives us a likeness to Christ as the stamp of the Father.[131] We are configured with Christ by spiritual character, which is the sacrament and reality of baptism, confirmation, and ordination. St Paul says that those whom God has predestined are conformed to the image of his Son, who is himself the image of the Invisible God, and so is the stamp of his nature.[132]

Character is like a stamp or seal set on someone. The wax with which letters used to be sealed was stamped with some design or letter (character) that was the distinctive mark of the sender. Thus St John speaks of Christ as bearing the 'seal' of the Father, who sent him (Jn 6:27). St Paul twice speaks of 'the seal of the Holy Spirit', when he seems to refer to the sacrament of confirmation (2 Cor 1:22; Eph 1:13). We find the idea that those who belong to God are marked in a special way in Ezekiel 9:6, the man dressed in linen is told not to slay anyone who has a mark on him or her. Likewise, in Revelation 7:3, the

---

131. ST 3a 63, 1 ad 2.
132. Rom 8:29; cf. Col 1:15; Heb 1:3.

angel is told not to harm anyone until 'we have sealed the servants of our God upon their foreheads'. These servants, it says, are marked for the enjoyment of eternal glory. The seal (*sphragis* in Greek) is impressed in us by the Holy Spirit.

The character received by these three sacraments (baptism, confirmation and ordination) is, then, the character of Christ, in whose priesthood all the faithful share, whether it is by the common priesthood of the faithful or the ordained ministry. As the liturgy of the Church shares in the worship which Christ our High Priest offers to his Father, so the sacraments which bestow character enable us to take part in the worship of the Church. As Colman O'Neill puts it, character enables the baptised to take part in the visible actions of the Church, in which Christ the High Priest is the principal agent.[133] Similarly, St Thomas Aquinas says that character disposes the soul for performing actions of divine worship.[134] Character is primarily bestowed for acts of divine worship rather than for receiving grace.[135]

Character is, to use the phrase of Fr McCabe, 'the mystery of the Church' of these three sacraments, because they relate us in a certain way to the Church and expressly order us for worship and service in the Church. We might say that they give us our position in the Church. For example, we cannot actively take part in the liturgy of the Church or receive any of the other sacraments without first being baptised. Confirmation is required for receiving

133. *Meeting Christ in the Sacraments*, p.115.
134. ST 3a 63, 4 ad 1.
135. C. O'Neill, op. cit., p.93.

the sacraments of holy orders and matrimony. Holy orders clearly define the position of certain men in the Church, who lead the faithful as their shepherds and offer sacrifice for the people. The Catechism says that these three sacraments remain for ever in a Christian 'as a vocation to divine worship and to the service of the Church'.[136] They cannot be repeated, St Thomas says, just as an altar can only be consecrated once.[137]

Following St Thomas, Fr Schillebeeckx sees baptism, confirmation and ordination as three steps, or degrees, of participating in the priesthood of Christ.[138] St Thomas explains this threefold distinction of sacramental character as follows: character is a signing (*signaculum*) by which one of the faithful is set aside (*deputed*) '*for the receiving and handing on*' to others what belongs to the worship of God. And sacramental character is appointed especially for this. In the same passage he continues:

> But the whole rite of the Christian religion is derived from the priesthood of Christ. Hence it is clear that sacramental character is especially the character of Christ, to whose priesthood the faithful are configured by sacramental characters, which are nothing other than certain participations in the priesthood of Christ, derived from Christ himself.[139]

Note that St Thomas here speaks of characters in the plural. He divides the three degrees of participation in the priesthood of Christ by character in the following way: we are set aside for divine worship either as we *receive or give*

---

136. CCC 1121
137. ST 3a 63, 5.
138. Op. cit., p.157.
139. ST 3a 63, 3.

gifts. Baptism is for receiving, confirmation and orders for giving. Christ's action in baptism is applied to someone *as an individual*, but character is bestowed by confirmation and ordination for applying Christ's power *to others*. St Thomas says that divine worship consists in receiving and handing on divine things. The power to do this is either a passive one for receiving or an active one for giving. Thus character implies a spiritual *power*.[140] Baptism is for the inner conversion and renewal of the individual person. It is the basis of the other sacraments. Confirmation is for professing one's faith *before others*, and ordination is for the service of others in the Church. Scheeben, however, thought that Aquinas only partly captured the meaning of character when he said that it sets someone aside for divine worship. Scheeben saw character more widely as a seal which *really* gives the Christian his or her dignity and vocation.[141]

We see that Christ meant his disciples to pass on gifts to others, because he committed the saving mission, which he had received directly from his heavenly Father, to the Apostles, who received the Spirit of Jesus.[142] On the day Christ arose from the dead, he passed on to the Apostles the power of sanctifying others by breathing on them the Holy Spirit, just as God breathed the breath of natural life into the first Adam at his creation.[143] The Apostles then handed on this active power to their successors by the sacrament of Orders, which consists in the laying on

---

140. ST 3a 63, 2.
141. *The Mysteries of Christianity*, p.588.
142. CCC 1120.
143. John 20:21-23; cf. Gen 2:7.

of hands as the sign of imparting the Holy Spirit.[144]

Since character, by definition, gives to all the faithful a share in the priesthood of Christ, we should now say a little about the difference between the general priesthood of the faithful and the priesthood of the ordained minister. The simplest way of discovering this difference is to look up the *Catechism of the Catholic Church*, paragraphs 1142 and 1546-1547, which tells us that not all the members of the community have the same function. The faithful are 'consecrated to be a holy priesthood' by baptism and confirmation. As St Peter says, the baptised are 'a royal priesthood, a people set apart' for the worship of God, 'to proclaim the wonderful deeds of him who called you out of darkness into light' (1 Pet 2:9). The ordained, ministerial priesthood is 'at the service of the common priesthood' of the faithful.[145] As the Catechism says, some members are called to the special service of the community, for which they are specially chosen by God and consecrated by a special sacrament, holy orders. Through this sacrament, the Holy Spirit enables the ordained minister to act in the person of Christ for the service of all the members of the Church.[146] Since he represents Christ, the ordained minister is an 'icon' of Christ. Only the ordained minister is a shepherd of the faithful. The ordained priesthood also guarantees that it is Christ who acts in the sacraments through his Holy Spirit.[147]

The difference between the common and ordained priesthood is described further by Edward Schillebeeckx.

144. CCC 1087.
145. CCC 1546-47.
146. CCC 1142.
147. CCC 1120.

The sacrament of ordination, he says, is for 'the priesthood of the apostolic office or episcopate'.[148] As successors of the Apostles, bishops have authority over the preaching of the word and the ministration of the sacraments. Thus the ordained ministry is connected with the authority, which Christ passed on to his Apostles at his ascension. The ordained priest receives a commission to act in the person of Christ. As Schillebeeckx expresses this, 'the acts of the priest are the personal acts of Christ himself made visible in sacramental form.'[149] 'The presbyterate is a participation in the priesthood of authority' or of the apostolic office.[150] Bishops confer on priests a partial share in their office, for priests can only exercise their ministry subject to a bishop. Although a priest can only act with a bishop, he receives his power to celebrate Mass *directly* from God; he is not just a delegate of the bishop. According to the teaching of the Second Vatican Council, bishops receive the fullness of the sacrament of Orders. Through their ordination, priests and deacons have a special aptitude for assisting the bishop in the teaching of the faith. As we have already noted, instruction in the faith is part of every sacrament and done through the liturgy of the word, which forms part of every sacrament. The priest is, in Schillebeeckx's phrase, 'the sacramental Christ': that is, he represents Christ in bodily form.[151] In this way the priesthood of the ordained minister differs from the common priesthood of the faithful.

148. *Christ the Sacrament*, p.169.
149. Ibid., p.171.
150. Ibid., p.172.
151. Ibid., p.212.

As we noted above, St Thomas calls character a spiritual power. The characters of all three sacraments are directed towards *activity* in the Church. Baptism and confirmation enabled the faithful to participate in the liturgy.[152] The liturgy itself is an exercise of the priesthood of Christ, who continually offers himself to the Father.[153] Christ acts directly in the liturgy, for he is present in it: 'To accomplish so great a work [of sanctifying men and women by the power of the Holy Spirit], Christ is always present in the Church, especially in the liturgical celebrations'.[154] He is present in none of these more so than in the sacrifice of the Mass. As character perfects the faithful for the worship of God, it perfects us for offering the worship which Christ offered to his Father.[155] He offered this worship especially on the Cross. Thus divine worship consists principally in the Mass, as it is the sacrifice of the Church.[156] The sacrament of Orders enables the ordained priest to offer the sacrifice for the people.

Let us sum up this section on sacramental character. Christians are specially signed, or marked, for the service of God, as soldiers were marked in the ancient times with the sign of their general or ruler.[157] Character gives a right and duty to take part in the worship of the Church. All character is directed to sacred actions in the worship of God by a royal priesthood, set apart for this very purpose.

---

152. CCC 1119.
153. CCC 1070.
154. SC 7.
155. ST 3a 62, 5; 63, 1.
156. ST 3a 63, 6.
157. ST 3a 63, 1.

Character is the 'reality and sacrament' of the three sacraments which cannot be repeated, since these three give their recipients a visible relation to the Church. They all give entry into the service of the Church. Baptism incorporates us into the Church, and confirmation and orders give a commission to carry on the saving mission, which Christ received from his Father and handed on to the Apostles.

Chapter Ten
Why We Need the Sacraments

The sacraments are one of the most distinctive aspects of the life of the Catholic Church. Yet many people, even with some Christian faith, see little need of them; some of them think that we can have purely spiritual access to God just by faith. Others, belonging to the ecclesial bodies of the Reformation, only accept the two principal sacraments, baptism and the Eucharist, but do not count the others as sacraments, because they do not find them clearly described in the New Testament. How are we to answer those who question the need to receive the sacraments? It may thus be useful to give here a list of reasons why sacraments are an essential part of the Christian religion. Although some of these reasons have already been mentioned, it may help to see them all together in an order.

1. We are not saved by faith and hearing of the word of God alone. We also need signs, because we are body and soul. Thus sacraments consist of words and signs. They touch the body through their sensible signs and are believed by the soul through hearing the words of the sacrament.[158]

2. God comes to meet us in our way, suited to our human nature. As our nature consists of a unity of body and soul, our contact with God is not purely spiritual or

---

158. Aquinas, ST 3a 60, 6.

mental, by faith alone, but also through corporeal signs, which are visible and tangible to us. These signs are the sacraments.

3. The Son of God became man by his incarnation, so that he could lead human beings back to God through his humanity, by which he is the Way to the Father (Jn 14:6). Thus the means of our salvation include actions and symbols, which can be grasped by the bodily senses. As God became man, our communication with God is not purely spiritual but also bodily through corporeal signs. As Christ, the Word made flesh, made his humanity the source of grace, 'full of grace and truth' (Jn 1:14), so grace now comes to us through the corporeal signs of the sacraments. Although Christ withdrew his body from the Earth at his ascension, we still have bodily access to him through the signs of the sacraments. Our communication with other human beings is bodily: this is the way we communicate as human persons. Colman O'Neill remarks that, through the incarnation, God encounters us in a human way by corporeal contact.[159]

4. As Christ said that his miracles of physical healing were accompanied by the spiritual healing of having sins forgiven (Mk 2:10; Jn 5:14), so he continues to heal us interiorly through the visible, tangible signs of the sacraments. Much healing is started by external means (medicines) but the healing occurs *within.*

5. As Schillebeeckx observes, we do not have *personal* contact with God by *nature,* but only through grace.[160]

---

159. *Meeeting Christ in the Sacraments*, p.88.
160. *Christ the Sacrament*, p.4.

Grace comes to us through the sacraments, because it comes to us through the *humanity* of Christ, united to his divine nature, which is the source of grace. We need the sacraments to come to share in the life of the Trinity because, just as God came down to us by the incarnation of his Son, so we come to God through the humanity of his Son.

6. By his death Christ provided, as it were, a medicine which could heal people of sin for all time. But a medicine does not actually cure anyone unless it is taken by individuals. Likewise, Christ only saves us individually. Each person needs to accept his atoning death with faith by receiving the sacraments (cf. Rom 3:25). They are our way of accepting his death. Christ has done enough to save everyone once for all, but the work of redemption still needs to be completed in us, one by one.

[handwritten margin note: PEOPLE MUST HELP THEMSELF?]

7. We also need the sacraments to be bonded together in a community, as we can only be saved in the name of the one true religion.[161] We are bonded together by external signs and actions. The members of religions without sacraments do not make a community with a definite structure like the Church.

8. We are incorporated into the Church, which is the mystical Body of Christ, as members who share his life, through the corporeal signs of the sacraments. They unite us with Christ, because they unite us to the Church.

9. Vorgrimler remarks that the sacraments are necessary for salvation, because there are not parallel roads to salvation. St Thomas Aquinas says that no one can be

---

161. Aquinas, ST 3a 61,1.

sanctified after sin except by Christ; thus we need to use the means of sanctification instituted and left by him, in which he continues to work through the power of the Holy Spirit. No one can be sanctified except by Christ, because he is the Sender of the Holy Spirit.

10. We do not achieve union with Christ just by our own moral effort and strength but primarily by the sanctifying grace, which comes to us through the sacraments. Indeed, sanctifying grace is the foundation of our moral life, since we need the help of grace to act virtuously. The cause of our sanctification is the Passion of Christ, which is applied to us by the sacraments.[162]

To gather these points together: as we are not justified by faith alone but also by baptism, so we are not only saved by hearing the word of God but also require the sacraments, which translate God's word into action and inwardly transform us (point 1). As the divine life comes to us through the humanity of Christ, who is both God and man, so we come to share in the divine life, which is the life of the three persons of the Trinity, through being made members of Christ's body (points 3 and 5). We become members of Christ, sharing in his life, by being incorporated into his mystical body, the Church, which is the sign of communion with God and of salvation in the world (*Lumen Gentium* 1, and point 8). Since we are not just spirit but a unity of body and soul, we need to be part of the body of Christ in order to receive the Spirit of Christ, and so share in the life of the Trinity.

---

162. ST 3a 60, 3.

TWO: THE SEVEN SACRAMENTS

Chapter One
Introduction

The number of the sacraments as seven was not fixed until the Second Council of Lyons in 1274.[163] We may, then, ask why there are just seven sacraments and no more or less. The first reason is that given by St Thomas Aquinas: as we are a unity of body and soul, so our spiritual life corresponds with our natural, bodily life.[164] As there are certain decisive stages in the life of everyone, like birth, reaching maturity, choosing a vocation, illness and death, so there is a sacrament of rebirth, one for maturing of faith, one of nourishment, which our natural life continually needs, one for dying and so on. In this way, our own living and dying is inserted into the life, death and resurrection of Christ. We may also note that our human life is perfected in us as an individual interiorly and in relation to a community or society: thus there is a mystery of grace and a mystery of the Church in every sacrament.

For Schillebeeckx, the seven sacraments correspond with seven 'psychologically meaningful' moments in human life: birth, growth, nourishment, marriage, a holy vocation, illness or death, healing and restoring broken friendship (the sacrament of reconciliation or penance when we break our friendship with God by sin). Let us

163. ND 28.
164. ST 3 65, 1.

go through these decisive stages in human life one by one. First, baptism is spiritual regeneration, being reborn by the Holy Spirit. The Holy Spirit is given again in confirmation for strength so that a person may grow fully in the faith, and face new challenges to that faith. The Eucharist preserves our spiritual power by nourishing us. The Eucharist is spiritual food, which we need to sustain us on our journey through this world to our homeland in heaven. Penance provides a cure for those who are spiritually infirm. The anointing of the sick is for those who are infirm in body, and prepares them for final glory in the next life. Lastly, there are two sacraments, which perfect us for our position in the community of the Church. By holy orders a man is enabled to offer sacrifice for the people. In marriage, the natural duty to continue the human race is raised to a sacrament, and so to a means of grace, as marriage signifies the union of Christ and his Bride, the Church.

When we further ask why these seven sacraments and not other rites, like blessing with holy water or the coronation of kings and queens, we notice that what distinguishes the seven sacraments is that they alone *apply the Passion of Christ* to us. How does this work out for each of the sacraments? In baptism, we die with Christ to sin and are buried with him. The Eucharist is itself the memorial of Christ's passion and death. The sacrament of penance forgives us our sins, just as Christ won the forgiveness of sins by the sacrifice of himself on the Cross. Likewise, anointing of the sick unites someone with the suffering of Christ and brings forgiveness of sins. By receiving Orders, a priest is united with Christ in the offering of his sacrifice, which won forgiveness of sins for the world. Marriage is a sign of the love which Christ showed for his Bride, the Church, by giving himself up for her on the Cross. The only sacrament for which it seems difficult to show that it applies the Passion of Christ is confirmation. Yet we can say that Christ could not pour out the Holy Spirit until he had first died and been glorified. So here too the giving of the Holy Spirit follows the Passion of Christ. St Thomas says that all the sacraments provide a remedy for sin, as the grace they give restores our human nature, which is wounded by sin.

The seven sacraments can conveniently be divided into three groups. First come the three *sacraments of initiation*: baptism, confirmation and the Eucharist. These complete one's incorporation into the Church. The end of being incorporated into the Church is to have union with Christ through receiving the sacrament of his life-giving Body and Blood. These three sacraments are common to everyone who receives the fullness of the Christian life. Next come the *sacraments of healing* for when our life in body or soul is impaired. Penance restores our communion with the Church when it is weakened or broken by sin; the anointing of the sick is for healing body and soul, so that one is restored to full life in the Church. The remaining two are the *sacraments of mission or vocation*: marriage and ordination.

As we have already noted, all the other sacraments are directed to the Eucharist, which is the source and culmination of the Church's life.[165] We cannot receive the Eucharist without first being incorporated into the Church by baptism. Confirmation marks maturity of

---

165. LG 11.

the spiritual life, which is nourished by the Eucharist. Penance and anointing of the sick restore one to full life in the Church when cut off from her by sin or illness. Marriage is a sign of the union between Christ and the Church, which is the effect of the Eucharist. As a man and woman are united bodily in marriage, so we are united with Christ by receiving his Body in the Eucharist. Holy orders is required for consecrating the Eucharist, and is also shared by deacons who assist priests and bishops.

We find a useful summary of the sacraments and their relation to one another in *Lumen Gentium*, paragraph 11, which tells us that the Church is brought into being through the sacraments. I shall briefly give the contents of this paragraph here. We are incorporated into the Church by baptism, and bound more perfectly to her by confirmation.

By baptism, we are set apart for divine worship and receive the duty to profess the faith of the Church. Confirmation equips us to spread and defend this faith better as witnesses to Christ.

In the Eucharist we offer the divine victim to God, as he offered himself to the Father on the cross in the perfect worship of God. The Eucharist is also the sign of the unity of the Church through communion.

By penance, we are reconciled with the Church and receive God's mercy, which God showed us by giving up his only Son for us on the cross.

The anointing of the sick enables people to unite themselves with the passion and death of Christ.

Through ordination, priests and deacons feed the Church by preaching the word of God and being stewards of God's grace in administering the sacraments.

The sacrament of Matrimony makes married couples a sign of the unity and love which exists between Christ and his Bride, the Church. From their union are born the children who become new members of the Church through baptism. The faithful family is like the Church in miniature: the Catechism calls the Catholic family 'the domestic church'.[166] The sacraments are the means by which all the faithful grow in the holiness, to which everyone is called, for, as the Second Vatican Council taught, holiness is the first vocation of everyone in the Church.[167]

---

166. CCC 1656.
167. LG 40, 2.

Chapter Two

Baptism

Baptism is the gateway to the sacraments (*ianua sacramentorum*), because we cannot receive any of the other sacraments without first having been baptised, and we cannot enter heaven without baptism.[168] As Christ said to Nicodemus, the one who came to be enlightened by him in the middle of the night, 'Unless you are born again of water and the Spirit, you cannot enter the kingdom of God' (Jn 3:5).

The first sacrament is prefigured in the Old Testament by the waters at creation, over which the Spirit hovered (Gen 1:2); by the flood, from which Noah was saved in the ark (Gen 6:11-8:12); and by the crossing of the Red Sea, the first of God's acts of redemption (Ex 14). St Peter, in the New Testament, calls the salvation of Noah by the ark an 'antitype' of baptism (1 Pt 3:21). As Noah was saved by the wood of the ark, so Christians are saved by the wood of the Cross. St Ambrose, in his instructions to the catechumens in Milan, taught that the flood and the crossing of the Red Sea were figures of baptism.[169]

Baptism is also prefigured by the cure of Naaman, the Syrian, from leprosy in the river Jordan (2 Kgs 5). His leprosy is an image of sin, which is taken away by baptism.

168. CCC 1213.
169. *De Sacramentis* I 5, 19.

Baptism is prefigured by circumcision, the mark for males of belonging to the chosen people, Israel.[170] Baptism gives us entry into the Church, which is the true Israel. The prophets too foretell baptism with the promise of a new heart when the people have been washed with water (Ez 36:25-27).

St Ambrose said that Christ established the 'form' of baptism when he was baptised in the river Jordan, and St Thomas Aquinas that this sacrament was instituted at the baptism of Christ.[171] Christ's baptism, however, was preceded by the baptism of St John the Baptist. John's baptism was only a baptism of repentance: that is, it was a sign of repentance, preceded by a confession of sins (Mk 1:5). John's baptism was a baptism of water, but Jesus' baptism is a baptism of the Holy Spirit (Matt 3:11; Mk 1:8). The sign of this difference between the two baptisms is that when Jesus let himself be baptised by John, 'in order to fulfil all righteousness' (Matt 3:15), the Holy Spirit visibly descended on Jesus in the form of a dove. The dove was a sign of the reconciliation of mankind with God, just as the dove was a sign of peace to Noah as the flood receded. The Holy Spirit rested on the One whom the Baptist pointed out as 'the Lamb of God who takes away the sin of the world' (Jn 1:29, 32). The sin of the world is original sin, which Christ took away by letting himself by sacrificed as a Passover Lamb.

We learn about the effects of baptism from the details of Christ's baptism, as recorded in the Gospels. The

---

170. Cf. Col 2:11-12.
171. ST 3a 66, 2.

heavens were opened to show us that people could now enter heaven, which had been closed since Adam and Eve were driven out of Paradise for their sin. But they could only enter heaven when Christ had died on the cross. His baptism was a sign of the effects of dying with Christ in baptism. Although Christ instituted the sacrament of baptism at his baptism, it only received its effect from Christ's passion and death, by which he gained for us the forgiveness of sin. Paul Haffner, however, thinks that baptism also had its effect before Christ's death.[172] Christ's baptism pointed towards his death, as it showed the effects of his Passion and death: the remission of sin and entry into heaven. Jesus indicated that his Passion was his second baptism when he said, 'I came to cast fire on earth... I have a baptism to be baptised with' (Lk 12:49). Baptism incorporates us into the mystery of Christ, because it associates us with his baptism and passion and death. Père Durrwell remarks that the baptism of Christ does not just prefigure the effects of his Passion but also of his resurrection because the Holy Spirit came down on Christ when he *rose* from the water.[173] Christ could only sanctify others when he had himself been consecrated and glorified by his death, because only then could he pour out the Holy Spirit (cf. Jn 7:39).

Although some have tried to trace baptism back to pagan cults, Bernard Neunheuser insists that it was instituted by Christ himself.[174] The evidence for its institution by

---

172. *The Sacramental Mystery*, p.32.
173. *The Resurrection*, p.314.
174. *Baptism and Confirmation*, p.40.

Christ lies in Luke 3:16: 'one greater than me comes after me; he will baptise you with the Holy Spirit and fire', and in Jesus' command to the Apostles to baptise all nations (Mt 28:19). Christ said that he came to baptise 'with the Holy Spirit and fire' (Mt 3:11). This fire could either mean tribulation or the Holy Spirit, who descended in tongues of fire at Pentecost.[175] It seems from Acts 1:5 'John baptized with water, but before many days you shall be baptized with the Holy Spirit', that the Apostles were baptised at Pentecost, but Haffner thinks that they were baptised with water.[176] Christ's baptism is a baptism of the Holy Spirit. When Peter had finished preaching at Pentecost, a large number of people were baptised and *received the Holy Spirit* (Acts 2:38). When St Paul came to Ephesus and found some disciples who said that they had received John's baptism but had not heard of the Holy Spirit, he baptised them in the name of Jesus and the Holy Spirit came down on them as he laid his hands on them (Acts 19:2-6).

The Symbolism of Water

The word 'baptise' comes from the Greek word *baptizein* which means to dip into water, to immerse, as sheep are dipped in a pool for cleansing in the autumn. Water is used as a sign in baptism, because baptism washes sin away and regenerates a person to new life.[177] Water symbolises death and life, for water both destroys in a flood and brings new

---

175. ST 3a 66, 3 ad 1.
176. Op. cit., p.32.
177. ST 3a 66, 3.

life to arid ground by causing seeds to germinate and spring up into new plants. All plants depend on water for having life. The Catechism describes the two principal effects of baptism as the destruction of sin and spiritual regeneration.[178] These two effects mirror the words of St Peter at Pentecost: 'Repent, and be baptised everyone of you in the name of Jesus Christ for the forgiveness of your sins; and you shall receive the gift of the Holy Spirit' (Acts 2:38). By being immersed in water at baptism, a person dies to sin and is buried with Christ. The result of this is that he or she rises to new life in Christ, just as he rose from the dead (Rom 6:3-4). The new life is the life which the Holy Spirit gives us: it is a spiritual life. St Basil the Great says that baptism destroys sin so that we may live by the Holy Spirit and bear the fruit of holiness.[179] His contemporary, St Gregory Nazianzen, says that the effect of baptism depends on the power of him who fills the water with his presence. Gregory Nazianzen established that when Christ descended into the river Jordan for his baptism, he blessed the water of the whole world.[180] We see the sense of this when we consider all the water in the world as one continuous mass, for all the oceans are joined and the rain that falls on the earth has first been taken up into the sky from the surface of the seas and oceans. Thus all water is one with the water in which Christ immersed himself in the River Jordan at his baptism. St Ephraim of Syria said that the Holy Spirit comes upon the

---

178. CCC 1262.
179. *De Spiritu Sancto* 15, 35.
180. *Oration* 40.

water at baptism as the Spirit hovered over the waters at creation.[181]

Baptism was seen in the early Church from the beginning as a washing with water and a bath. St Paul refers to baptism when he says that Christ cleansed the Church 'by the washing of water and with the word' (Eph 5:26). He calls baptism 'a washing' again, writing to the Corinthians: 'you were washed, you were sanctified, you were justified in the name of the Lord Jesus and in the Spirit of our God' (1 Cor 6:11). The paralysed man waited by the pool of Bethsaida many years, waiting to get into the water first to be healed (Jn 5:2). Jesus told the man born-blind to go and wash in the pool of Siloam after he had received back his sight (Jn 9:11). Thus baptism is a washing and an illumination, for it brings the light of faith to the mind, which had earlier been obscured in darkness by the effect of sin. This is how St Justin, who was martyred in Rome c. 165, describes baptism: as a washing, a rebirth and an illumination (*photismos*).[182] Aquinas says that baptism does not have to be done by immersion in a pool but can be by effusion, that is, by pouring water on the head of the candidate, which is the customary practice in the Western Church now. But he says that immersion better expresses being buried with Christ.[183] He also held that it does not have to be a triple immersion but one is sufficient.[184] Triple immersion was for the threefold name of the Trinity. But with effusion, water should be poured

---

181. *Hymn* 8, 16.
182. *First Apology* 61, 65.
183. ST 3a 66, 7.
184. ST 3a 66, 8.

on the head three separate times, once for each name of the Trinity. St Cyril of Jerusalem, in his catechesis at the end of the fourth century, saw in the triple immersion a symbol of the three days which Christ spent in the tomb.

The Effects of Baptism

Baptism is the first sacrament of the *forgiveness of sins*: in the Nicene Creed it says, 'I confess one baptism for the forgiveness of sins'. Baptism washes away the guilt of original sin, which we inherit from Adam, and of all previous sins. Penance is the second sacrament of forgiveness, for sins committed after baptism. There is no need of confession of sins before baptism, because it is a dying with Christ: it is the burial of the old, natural self and the birth of the new, spiritual person. Thus one can only be baptised once, just as one can only be born and die once.[185] The purpose of dying with Christ is so that one may live a new life, according to the Spirit.

> We were buried with him by baptism into death, so that as Christ was raised from the dead by the glory of the Father, we too might walk in newness of life (Rom 6:4).

St Cyril of Jerusalem explains that we do not literally die and rise with Christ in baptism but only symbolically, or we might say spiritually. St Cyril says that baptism is 'an imitation in an image'.[186] Through baptism we share in Christ's sufferings by an imitation, not in truth. St Paul says that we are conformed with Christ 'in a likeness of his death' in baptism (Rom 6:5). The translation of the Revised

---

185. ST 3a 66, 9.
186. *Mystagogic Catecheses* 2, 5.

Standard Version obscures this point by translating 'in a likeness' (*en homoiomati*) merely as 'like'. In the sacrament we die with Christ in a likeness, as immersion in water is a likeness of being buried with him. But, St Cyril adds, although we die with Christ in a sacramental likeness in baptism, the salvation which baptism brings is not just a likeness but *real*. St Ambrose, in the West, likewise said that, as Christ died, so the baptized person dies to sin, not in reality but in a likeness.[187]

As baptism is a likeness of Christ's death and resurrection, symbolised by descending into and rising from the waters, so another effect of baptism is to be *conformed with Christ in his death and resurrection*. St Basil asks how we can imitate Christ and answers: 'By being buried with him in baptism'.[188] St Paul brings out clearly the steps in the argument: 'All of us who have been baptised into Christ Jesus were baptised into his death. We were buried therefore with him by baptism into death' (Rom 6:3-4). In the next verse, he draws the consequence: if we are united with Christ in his death, we shall also be united with him in his resurrection (Rom 6:5). We die to sin in order to live for God (Rom 6:10-11). St Ambrose saw baptism as a Passover, that is, a crossing over, from sin to life. St Thomas Aquinas' line of thought was that we are conformed with Christ's death and resurrection because by baptism we are conformed with Christ's baptism, which pointed towards his death.[189] Christ's death and

---

187. *De Sacramentis* II 7, 23.
188. *De Spiritu Sanctu* 15, 35.
189. ST 3a 72, 1 ad 3.

resurrection were his Passover to the Father. Jesus spoke of his death as a second baptism, after his baptism in the River Jordan, when he asked James and John 'Can you be baptised with the baptism with which I must be baptised?' (Mk 10:38).

As we die with Christ in baptism in order to rise to a new life, so the next effect of baptism is *rebirth in the Holy Spirit*: as Christ said, we are born again by water and the Holy Spirit (Jn 3:5). St Thomas Aquinas says that baptism was instituted in order to generate people for spiritual life.[190] For St Ambrose, baptism regenerates us to grace as water generates living things to life.[191] Among the effects of baptism, St Cyril of Jerusalem numbers the gift of the Holy Spirit and the grace of adoption as children of God.[192] Likewise, St Ambrose says that baptism gives us the grace of the Holy Spirit.[193] The spiritual rebirth of baptism brings about the indwelling of the Holy Spirit: 'Do you not know that you are God's temple and that God's Spirit dwells in you?'(1 Cor 3:16). The principle of new life in Christ is the Holy Spirit, whom Christ could only send after his death and resurrection. Thus we have to die and rise with Christ in baptism, in order to share in his Holy Spirit.

The consequence of being reborn by water and the Holy Spirit is that we are made *adopted sons and daughters of God* (Christ is the Son of God by nature). As adopted children of God, we are able to call God 'Father' in prayer,

---

190. ST 3a 69, 8.
191. *De Sacramentis* III 1, 3.
192. *Mystagogic Catecheses* 2, 6.
193. *De Sacramentis* I 6, 24.

just as Jesus taught his disciples in giving them the 'Our Father'. 'All who are led by the Spirit are sons of God', St Paul says (Rom 8:14). We witness that we are children of God when we pray to him as 'Father': 'When we cry "Abba, Father", the Spirit himself witnesses with our spirit that we are children of God' (Rom 8:15-16). We cannot call God 'Father' without implying faith in the Trinity, for we are sons of God because of the Son of God, who came to share our human nature, and we become sons and daughters by being reborn by the Holy Spirit. In one of the few verses in the New Testament which explicitly mentions the whole Trinity, St Paul wrote: 'Because you are sons, God has sent the Spirit of his Son into your hearts crying "Abba, Father"' (Gal 4:6). Our adoption as children of God is founded on the mystery of the incarnation, for we are reborn as children of God by the Holy Spirit, just as Christ's human nature was conceived in Mary by the power of the Holy Spirit. As Christ's human nature was conceived in Mary, so we are reborn children of God in the Church.

Christ was revealed as the Son of God at his baptism, so that we could see that one of the effects of baptism is to make us sons and daughters of God, when the voice of the Father said, 'This is my beloved Son, in whom I am well pleased' (Mt 3:17). For St Ambrose, not just the Holy Spirit but the whole Trinity is present in the water of baptism, because at Christ's baptism the Father spoke, the Son descended into the water and the Holy Spirit rested on him in the shape of a dove.[194] The Trinity

---

194. Ibid. I 5, 19.

is the principal cause of grace at baptism, St Thomas says, because, although it is Christ who baptises, he does nothing without the Father or the Holy Spirit: all three work together. One of the reasons why baptism is in the name of the Father, and of the Son, and of the Holy Spirit and not just in the name of God or of Christ, is that the whole Trinity was revealed at the baptism of Christ, St Thomas says. The other reason is that Christ commanded his Apostles to make 'disciples of all nations, baptising them in the name of the Father, and of the Son, and of the Holy Spirit' (Mt 28:19).[195]

Just as Jesus is called the Christ because he is the one anointed by the Holy Spirit, so another effect of baptism is that _we are made 'christs'_, that is, anointed ones. St Cyril of Jerusalem says that the baptised are 'christs' because they are anointed, just as Christ was anointed with the oil of gladness (Ps 44:8).[196] In explaining that the additional rites of baptism are not necessary but add to the solemnity of baptism, for nothing is superfluous which instructs us about the interior effects of the sacraments, St Thomas says that we are signed with chrism after the washing with water so that we can be called 'christs'.[197] St Leo the Great points out that, because all baptised persons are anointed ones, or 'christs', they share in the royal priesthood of Christ, who is Priest, Prophet and King.[198]

Since we become sons and daughters of God in his Son, who shares our human nature, a further effect of baptism

---

195. ST 3a 66, 5.
196. *Mystagogic Catecheses* 3, 1.
197. ST 3a 66, 10 ad 2.
198. *Sermon* 4; (PL 54, 148).

is that we are *incorporated into the body of Christ* and are made members of the Church, which is the mystical body of Christ. All this is the work of the Holy Spirit: 'For by one Spirit you were all baptised into one body – Jews or Greeks, slaves or free – and all were made to drink of one Spirit' (1 Cor 12:13). Our incorporation into the body of Christ and the Church is completed by receiving the Eucharist, which is the sacrament of Christ's Body and Blood.

The consequence of being buried with Christ in baptism and being regenerated as children of God by the Holy Spirit is *the renewal of our human nature*. St Thomas Aquinas says that Christ's human nature was conceived by the power of the Holy Spirit, because he came to renew our human nature.[199] The renewal of our nature goes with being regenerated by the Holy Spirit: 'he saved us in virtue of his mercy, by the washing of regeneration and renewal in the Holy Spirit' (Tit 3:5). St Paul expresses the renewal of our human nature by saying we 'put on Christ': 'All who are baptised in Christ have clothed yourselves in Christ' (Gal 3:27). We have put off the old, natural self and put on the new self: 'You have stripped off your old behaviour with your old self and have put on a new self which will progress towards true knowledge as it is renewed in the image of the Creator' (Col 3:8-10). St Paul continues the image of clothing in drawing the moral consequence of baptism, which is imitating Christ: 'Be clothed in compassion, kindness and humility, gentleness and patience' (Col 3:11). Our human nature is renewed

---

199. ST 2a 2ae 2, 8.

in the image of God and of Christ, who is himself the Image of God (Col 1:15). As we put on Christ, we are conformed to his likeness.[200]

The *Catechism of the Catholic Church* names three main effects of baptism. First baptism symbolises burial with Christ's death and rising with him as 'a new creation' (2 Cor 5:17; Gal 6:15). Secondly, baptism is the washing of regeneration and renewal by the Holy Spirit. Thirdly, it is enlightenment.[201] All these effects go together. Baptism works the forgiveness of sins because it is dying with Christ and the burial of the old self. St Thomas Aquinas even says that baptism gives us a share in the Passion of Christ 'as though the baptised person suffered and died', because baptism makes us members of Christ's body.[202] He explains that baptism removes the guilt of sin but not the consequences of the Fall, which everyone suffers in this life: namely the struggle against concupiscence (the desires of the flesh), sickness and death. These will only be completely taken away when our human nature is wholly restored with the resurrection of the body.[203] It is only the guilt of sin which is an obstacle to entering heaven and separates us from God. Since baptism takes away the liability to punishment for sin (*reatus poenae*), it opens the gates of heaven for us. St Augustine thought that the practice of baptising infants was a witness to the universal existence of original sin (with the exception of Our Lady and Christ's human nature), or why else would there be

---

200. Cyril of Jerusalem, *Mystagogic Catecheses* 3, 1.
201. CCC 1214-1216.
202. ST 3a 69, 2 ad 1.
203. ST 3a 69, 3.

a point in baptising them? He developed his doctrine about baptism against the Pelagians, because they saw no need for the baptism of infants, as they did not think that we inherit original sin by nature. Augustine held that it is possible to baptise infants, although they cannot yet make an act of faith, because the faith of their parents and sponsors supplies for them. Infants can also be baptised because we are not justified by our own explicit faith in the first place but by the imparting of the Holy Spirit, who is given in baptism.[204]

Secondly, the water that washes away our sins in baptism is also a sign of the living waters of the grace of the Holy Spirit. It is the Holy Spirit who enlightens our minds. St Peter, in the verse where he says that the faithful are a royal priesthood and a consecrated nation, set apart for the praises, that is the worship, of God, says that they have been called out of darkness into light (1 Pet 2:19). The Israelites were called out of darkness into light at the Exodus, which prefigured baptism, as they crossed through the waters of the Red Sea. Baptism is enlightenment, because it is the sacrament of faith, which enlightens the mind with the knowledge of things which we cannot know by natural reason alone but only by the light of grace. We see that baptism is the sacrament of faith, because it includes the threefold questioning of the candidate about belief in the Creed, which is itself Trinitarian in structure, as its articles are grouped under belief in the Father, in the Son and in the Holy Spirit.[205]

---

204. *Epistola* 98, 2.
205. ST 3a 66, 1 ad 1.

Through profession of faith in the Trinity and baptism in the name of the Trinity, this sacrament brings about our entry into the life of the Trinity.[206] By being adopted as children of God through being reborn by the Holy Spirit, we share in the Spirit of the Son, whom God sends into our hearts, crying 'Abba, Father' (Gal 4:6).

206. CCC 1239.

Chapter Three

Confirmation

In the early Church, confirmation seems to have formed one continuous rite with baptism. St Cyril of Jerusalem tells us that, after baptism, the candidates were anointed with myrrh (*muron*), just as Christ was anointed with the Holy Spirit (Acts 10:38).[207] Myrrh was an oil made fragrant with balsam, which we call chrism. The candidate was anointed with myrrh on the forehead and organs of sense (ears, eyes, mouth), and this was the seal of the Holy Spirit. 'Your body is anointed with visible myrrh, while your soul is sanctified by the life-giving Spirit'.[208] In the West, St Ambrose tells us that, following baptism, at the invocation of the priest the candidate received a spiritual signing, which was the sevenfold gift of the Holy Spirit.[209] St Augustine notes a similar practice: after the bath of water came the anointing with chrism, laying on of hands and a signing (*consignatio*). In the Eastern Church confirmation still follows baptism immediately even today. As we receive the Holy Spirit in baptism, one might wonder why there is a second sacrament for receiving the Holy Spirit. Why are baptism and confirmation two separate sacraments, and how did they eventually become separate in the Western

---

207. *Mystagogic Catecheses* 3, 2.
208. Ibid., 3, 3.
209. *De Sacramentis* III 2, 8.

Church? Let us begin with the evidence for confirmation in Scripture.

Confirmation in Scripture

One of the difficulties about this sacrament is that there does not appear to be much about it in the New Testament. We read in the Acts of the Apostles 8:14-17 that Peter and John laid their hands on some people of Samaria after they had been baptised, and they received the Holy Spirit. We also hear of 'the laying on of hands' after 'ablutions', that is the washing of baptism, in Hebrews 6:2. St Paul speaks of the 'seal' (*sphragis*) of the Holy Spirit in two texts: 'he has put his seal upon us and given us his Spirit in our hearts as a guarantee' (2 Cor 1:22), and 'In him you also ... were sealed with the promise of the Holy Spirit' (Eph 1:13). We recall that Christ (the Anointed) is the one on whom 'God the Father set his seal' (Jn 6:27). The Holy Spirit is the gift, whom Christ promised to send (Jn 14:26; 15:26). He is the promised gift whom the Messiah brings: as Jesus ascends, he tells the Apostles that he will send them 'the promise of the Father' (Lk 24:49). The Messiah is the one on whom the sevenfold gift of the Spirit of the Lord rests: the spirit of wisdom, understanding, counsel, fortitude, knowledge and fear of the Lord (fear is mentioned twice, Isa 11:2). The Holy Spirit prophesied by Isaiah descended on Christ at his baptism. St Luke says that Jesus began his public ministry by reading in the synagogue the passage of Isaiah, which says that the Spirit had anointed him to preach the Gospel to the poor (Lk 4:18; cf. Isa 61:1-2).

St Peter saw Joel's prophecy that God would pour out his Spirit on all flesh at the end of time fulfilled at

Pentecost (Acts 2:17-18; cf. Joel 2:28-29). Ezekiel too prophesied that God would put a new spirit in the hearts of the people of the New Covenant after they had been washed clean with water (Ez 36:25-26).

Bernard Neunheuser concluded that there was no evidence in the New Testament for a separate rite of anointing and sealing but that there was a single rite of initiation, which included the laying on of hands.[210] He identified confirmation with the laying on of hands, which was done by the Apostles at first. Yet confirmation seems to have been a different sacrament from baptism in the early Church, although they formed a continuous rite, because St Cyril of Jerusalem devotes a special catechesis to the anointing with myrrh, the third *Mystagogic Catechesis*, as we have noted above.

Confirmation in the Early Church

At first, the essential rite of confirmation in the East was the anointing with chrism, called 'chrismation', as we see from St Cyril of Jerusalem. But in the West, the essential rite was the laying on of hands. An anointing combined with the imposition of hands seems to go back to Pope Sylvester (314-335), who may have taken it from the *Apostolic Tradition*, which for long has been ascribed to Hippolytus, who was in Rome circa 220. Fr Schillebeeckx thinks that anointing with chrism may have been part of the apostolic rite.[211] St Ambrose calls confirmation

---

210. *Baptism and Confirmation*, p.51.
211. *Christ the Sacrament*, p.154.

a 'spiritual seal' (*signaculum spirituale*).[212] The new teaching in St Ambrose is that confirmation gives us *the seven gifts of the Holy Spirit*, which he names as: wisdom, understanding, counsel, courage, knowledge, piety and holy fear.[213] He calls them the seven 'virtues', or powers, of the Spirit. The sevenfold gift of the Spirit was also the purpose of the sacrament for Rabanus Maurus (d. 856), who was probably the author of the hymn *Veni, Creator Spiritus*.

Confirmation in the Middle Ages

Faustus, bishop of Riez in Southern France (d. 490), saw the difference between baptism and confirmation in that confirmation gives strength (*robur*). It was originally called confirmation, however, because it completes, or confirms, baptism. But *con-firmare* also means to make firm or strong. Faustus was responsible for the conception of confirmation as making us 'soldiers of Christ', ready for battle with the outward enemies of the Christian faith and to defend the Faith when attacked for it. This effect of confirmation was also promoted by Rabanus Maurus, bishop of Mainz in the ninth century.

Rabanus combined the teachings of St Ambrose and Faustus about confirmation. For Rabanus, confirmation strengthens us for bearing witness to, and preaching, the Faith because it gives us the sevenfold gift of the Spirit, just as the Holy Spirit came down visibly on Christ before he began to preach openly. The Holy Spirit also descended

---

212. *De Sacramentis* III 2.
213. Ibid., III 2, 8-10.

visibly on the Apostles at Pentecost, just before they began to preach the Gospel to the four corners of the world. Rabanus explained that chrism is used in confirmation because oil is a sign of abundance, richness and flowing over with good things in Scripture. Thus the fragrant oil of chrism is the sign of receiving the fullness of the gift of the Holy Spirit in confirmation. It is in this idea of receiving the fullness of the Holy Spirit that we can see the difference between baptism and confirmation, as will be explained further below.[214]

Peter Lombard (c. 1100-1150) established that the essential rite of confirmation consisted in the words used by the bishop in signing the recipient with chrism. This point was followed by Paul VI in his *Apostolic Constitution on Confirmation* of 1971. Peter Lombard distinguished the two sacraments by saying that the Spirit is given in baptism for the forgiveness of sins, and in confirmation for strength (*robur*), to strengthen one for action by sharing in the mission of the Church.[215] One might say that the Spirit is given simply in baptism for one's own *interior* transformation, but fully in confirmation for *external* witness and mission. These points of Peter Lombard frequently recur in the thought of theologians and the teaching of the Church in recent decades, as we shall see. The *Catechism of the Catholic Church*, for example, says that we are confirmed so that we may share more in the mission of the Church and in the fullness of the Holy Spirit. The essential rite, it says, consists in 'anointing

---

214. Cf. ST 3a 65, 1 ad 4.
215. *Sententiarum* IV dist. 7, 1 (PL 192, 855).

with chrism on the forehead'. The effect of confirmation is the full outpouring of the Holy Spirit, which gives one the power to profess the Christian faith publicly.[216]

Peter Lombard provided the basis for St Thomas Aquinas, who said that the sacraments are distinguished by being ordered to special effects of grace. Thus baptism is distinguished from confirmation because the Holy Spirit is given in baptism for the spiritual life simply.[217] But in confirmation we receive the perfect age of the spiritual life and an increase of grace, and are strengthened after baptism.[218] For St Thomas, confirmation is 'the sacrament of the plenitude of grace'.[219] Christ instituted this sacrament, he says, so that it might give us the plenitude of the Holy Spirit. But he instituted it by *promising* to send the Holy Spirit, which he could not give until after he had risen again and ascended to the Father. Christ promised to send the Holy Spirit when he said, 'When the Counsellor (Paraclete) comes, whom I shall send to you from the Father, even the Spirit of truth, who proceeds from the Father, he will bear witness to me; and you also are my witnesses' (Jn 15:26). Just as the Holy Spirit is one of the witnesses to Christ (cf. 1 Jn 5:6), so the gift of the Spirit strengthens us to be witnesses to Christ in confirmation. As the Catechism says, Christ, the Messiah, possessed the fullness of the Holy Spirit and it was part of the prophecies of the Old Testament in Ezekiel and Joel

---

216. CCC 1294, 1300, 1302, 1305.
217. ST 3a 72, 2 ad 2.
218. ST 3a 72, 1.
219. ST 3a 72, 1 ad 3, ad 4.

that he would give it to the whole people.[220]

Echoing the idea of Rabanus Maurus, Aquinas held that the fullness of the Holy Spirit is given to us for spiritual strength (*robur*).[221] The fullness of the Holy Spirit is signified by chrism, which is oil mixed with sweet smelling balsam. St Thomas does not count the laying on of hands but only the anointing with chrism as the essential rite of confirmation. He points out that the Messiah, or Christ, was so-called because he was the one anointed with the oil of gladness, according to the Psalms (44:7). Confirmation enables one to spread the Gospel by word and example.[222] It strengthens one for defending the Faith and combating the enemies of the Faith. It is not necessary for salvation, but it belongs to the *perfection* of salvation. As we have already seen, it is now required for the reception of holy orders and marriage.

The teaching of the Middle Ages about confirmation found an echo in the twentieth century. The Second Vatican Council taught that confirmation is for professing the Faith publicly. It deepens the grace of baptism and binds the recipient more closely to the Church.[223] Like Peter Lombard, the universal Catechism says that it helps us to share more in the mission of Jesus Christ.[224] Thus confirmation is the special sacrament for everyone in the Church who is involved in the work of catechising and evangelising.

---

220. CCC 1286-1287.
221. ST 3a 72, 2.
222. ST 3a 72, 5.
223. LG 11. Cf. CCC 1285.
224. CCC 1294.

Anointing or Laying on of Hands?

As we have already seen, there has been some unclarity throughout the ages about whether confirmation essentially consisted in the laying on of hands, as it seems to have been done by the Apostles, or in the signing of the candidate with chrism. It was this unclarity which Pope Paul VI set out to resolve definitively with his *Apostolic Constitution on the Sacrament of Confirmation (Divinae Consortium Naturae)* in 1971.

As the Catechism notes, the origin of the sacrament of confirmation was the laying on of hands.[225] But we hear of a signing with chrism in the early Church. St Paul too speaks of the 'seal of the Holy Spirit' (2 Cor 1:22), which seems to indicate a signing. Paul VI mentions that Christ promised that the Holy Spirit would help the Apostles to bear witness to him when they were persecuted: 'When they hand you over, do not worry about how to speak or what to say ... because it will not be you speaking, but the Spirit of your Father will speak in you' (Matt 10:20). As evidence for confirmation in the New Testament, Paul VI states, 'From that time (Pentecost) on, the Apostles, in fulfilment of Christ's wish, imparted the gift of the Spirit to the newly baptised by the laying on of hands to complete the grace of baptism' (cf. Acts 2:38).[226] Quoting *Lumen Gentium* 11, he adds: 'Through the sacrament of confirmation, those who have been born anew in baptism

---

225. CCC 1288. Cf. Acts 8:17.
226. Apostolic Constitution *Divinae consortium naturae* (1971) in *Documents of the Liturgy* (Liturgical Press, Collegeville 1982), DOL303 no. 2501.

receive the inexpressible Gift of the Holy Spirit himself, by which "they are endowed ... with special strength"'.[227]

Paul VI next gives a brief history of the rite of confirmation. In the West, the washing of baptism was followed by the anointing, laying on of hands and signing. Pope Innocent III (1198-1216) decreed that the laying on of hands is designated by anointing on the forehead, and this is called confirmation, because by it the Holy Spirit is given for growth and strength.[228] Innocent IV (1243-1254) affirmed that the Apostles conferred the Holy Spirit 'through the laying on of hands, which confirmation or anointing on the forehead represents'.[229] He thus equated confirmation with anointing with chrism, which represented the laying on of hands. The *Decree for the Armenians*, issued by the Council of Florence in 1439, quotes Acts 8:17 and states, 'in the Church confirmation is given in the place of the laying on of hands'.[230] In the eighteenth century, Benedict XIV reaffirmed that 'in the Latin Church the sacrament of confirmation is conferred by using sacred chrism or olive oil, mixed with balsam and blessed by the bishop, and by the tracing of the sign of the cross by the minister of the sacrament on the forehead of the recipient'.[231] Paul VI came to the conclusion that the most important element of confirmation in the East and West was the anointing with chrism, which represents the laying on of hands done by the Apostles. He thus determined that the anointing with chrism on the forehead

227. Ibid. DOL303, no. 2502.
228. DS 785.
229. Cf. Paul VI Apostolic Constitution DOL303 no. 2504.
230. ND 1417.
231. Paul VI, op. cit. DOL303, no. 2504.

is the essential sign, so that the rite of confirmation fittingly embraces the essence of the sacramental rite.

> The Sacrament of Confirmation is conferred through the anointing with chrism on the forehead, which is done by the laying on of the hand and through the words *"Accipe signaculum doni Spiritus Sancti"*.[232]

The Catechism says that the visible sign of anointing imprints 'a spiritual seal'.[233]

Pope Paul VI judged that the words used in the Church of the East better expressed the Gift of the Holy Spirit in confirmation. The form of words used in the West until 1971 were: "I sign you with the sign of the cross, and confirm you with the chrism of salvation. In the name of the Father, and of the Son, and of the Holy Spirit". But the essential words used in the East were simply *'signaculum doni Spiritus Sancti'* ('The seal of the Gift of the Holy Spirit'). Thus Paul VI confirmed the existing rite of anointing with chrism but adopted the formula of the East. He stated that the laying on of hands on the candidate, which is symbolised by the bishop holding up his arms outstretched during the prayer for the seven gifts of the Holy Spirit before the signing with chrism, does not belong to the essence of the sacramental rite but contributes to the integrity and perfection of the whole rite.

Why Two Separate Sacraments?

As we have already noted, confirmation was originally given straightaway after baptism in the early Church. This

---

232. Ibid. DOL303, no. 2507.
233. CCC 1293.

is still the practice in the Church of the East, and in the West when an adult is baptized at the Easter Vigil. How did the two sacraments become separated in the West, and what is the reason for having two sacraments which give the Holy Spirit?

Schillebeeckx sees the reason for two sacraments, baptism and confirmation, in the two visible missions of the Holy Spirit: at the baptism of Our Lord the Holy Spirit descended on Christ in the form of a dove, and at Pentecost he came down on Mary and the Apostles, the first members of the Church, as tongues of fire. There are two sacraments for Schillebeeckx, because the Church was *established* at Pentecost, although born when blood and water flowed from Christ's side on the Cross. Confirmation, then, exists for establishing someone in power: someone who has only received baptism, Schillebeeckx says, has not yet been established in power.[234] Likewise, Colman O'Neill saw baptism and confirmation as corresponding to the mysteries of Easter and Pentecost. We are incorporated into the mystery of Christ's death and resurrection by baptism. This is completed by confirmation, just as the mission of the Son, which reached its high point in his death and resurrection, was completed by the mission of the Holy Spirit at Pentecost.[235] The Catechism says that confirmation 'perpetuates the grace of Pentecost'.[236]

For Paul Haffner too, the effect of confirmation is that it completes baptism. As the beginning of Christ's public

---

234. *Christ the Sacrament* p.200.
235. *Meeting Christ in the Sacraments*, p.151.
236. CCC 1288.

ministry was marked by the descent of the Holy Spirit on him at his baptism, so the Apostles had to wait to be clothed with power from on high at Pentecost before they could go out into the whole world and preach the Gospel.[237] At Pentecost, the Apostles were transformed into missionaries who took the Gospel everywhere. Thus Haffner says that confirmation, which is the sacrament of Pentecost, so to speak, endows one with a mission in the Church. In his view, baptism is given for the Christian as an individual, and confirmation for the Christian as a public witness to the Faith and a co-worker in the mission of the Church. This was also the view of Colman O'Neill, that confirmation gives one a share in the mission of the Church as an adult. O'Neill distinguished between the effects of baptism and confirmation by saying that one receives the fruits of Christ's priesthood for oneself in baptism, and for bringing these fruits to others in confirmation. Confirmation enables one to take the fruits of Christ's priesthood to others.[238] Schillebeeckx calls confirmation 'the sacrament of the Apostolate'. Confirmation gives one strength for witnessing to Christ by preaching the Gospel by word and example, as the fullness of power, which was given to the Apostles at Pentecost, is lacking in one who has not yet been confirmed.

My own view about confirmation is that, although the sacrament is for giving one strength and a share in the mission of the Church, the teaching of it unjustly neglects the seven gifts of the Holy Spirit, for which the

237. Acts 1:8.
238. Op. cit., pp.155f.

bishop prays with outstretched arms before he signs the candidates with chrism. The seven gifts are only named in the *Catechism of the Catholic Church* 1831, without any more detail about what they are. When we know a little about what these seven gifts are, we shall see that they are of great practical benefit and that many constantly call them into play in their daily lives without ever being aware of them, although every confirmed person has received them. I shall, therefore, complete this account of confirmation with a brief description of the seven gifts of the Holy Spirit, which confirmation gives us.

In focussing on the activity and mission of the Church and her members, we easily tend to forget that it is individual persons who act, and that their action springs from the *inner* person. The gifts of the Holy Spirit are given for strengthening the inner person. One way that these gifts strengthen the person is that they harmonise his or her powers, so that they act in concert. They are both active, in that they prompt us to action, and passive, in that they make us docile to the promptings of the Holy Spirit. Acting with the inspiration of the seven gifts is like the difference between sailing in a boat with its sails driven by the wind and toiling at the oars in a rowing boat.

The highest of the gifts is Wisdom, which is the first in the order of the gifts taken from Isaiah 11:2. The gift of wisdom is connected with charity, since it helps us to love our Catholic faith and gives us a connaturality, or real sense, for the mysteries of our faith. Since wisdom is often shown in good judgement, it enables us to judge things spiritually. As St Paul says, it is the spiritual person who judges the things of the Spirit: only 'the spiritual person discerns spiritually' (1 Cor 2:14). With the gift of *Understanding*, we are enabled to penetrate the mysteries of faith, so that we do not just have obscure faith but the truths to which one assents with faith are in some degree illuminated by the Holy Spirit. The gift of *Knowledge* helps one to see how the works of creation manifest the Creator and to relate our scientific knowledge of the world to God as the author of everything we study with human reason. We need the gift of *Counsel*, so that we make good decisions in life and choose that kind of life which seeks the kingdom of God first and leads us to eternal beatitude. But in order to put into effect the decisions which we make with the influence of the gift of counsel, we also need the gift of *Fortitude* to have the courage to overcome the difficulties and opposition we shall encounter in witnessing to the Gospel of Christ in the world. It is the gift of fortitude which enables someone to persevere in the religious life, which has been chosen with the aid of the gift of counsel.

Where Isaiah repeats the gift of the fear of the Lord, this gift is divided by the Church into two: Piety and Fear. *Piety* does not so much mean being devout, as we commonly understand the word today, but comes from the old Roman quality of *pietas*, which meant the devotion of children to their parents. This is the gift then, which enables us to be children of God who have the confidence to call him 'Father' and want to please God. Other effects of this gift are that we worship God, trust in Providence, depend on God and grow in prayer. It is also the gift by which we have devotion for the truths of the faith, so that the loving heart perfects the intellect (for faith in itself is an act of the intellect). In the Old Testament, 'the fear of the Lord is the beginning of wisdom' (Ps 110:10). In Proverbs it also says: 'the fear of the Lord is a fountain of life' (Prov 14:27). With the gift of *Fear*, we fear to be separated from God and so want to avoid sin. We also fear the punishment of sin in eternity. This is a most necessary gift for today, when we see that so many despise the law of God, because they have no fear of God. If more people had the fear of God, there would be more order, and so peace and happiness, in society. St John of the Cross says that the perfect fear of a son proceeds from the perfect love of the Father.[239] Thus charity unites all the gifts of the Holy Spirit.

---

239. *The Spiritual Canticle* A XVII, 2.

Chapter Four
The Eucharist

The Eucharist is the third sacrament of initiation into the Church and her worship, and completes the process of Christian initiation. The purpose and end of being incorporated into the Church and of being strengthened with the Gift of the Holy Spirit in baptism and confirmation is to be united with Christ in communion through sharing in his life-giving Body and Blood in the Eucharist. In other words, the end of Christian initiation is *union with Christ*. In this chapter I want just to focus briefly on four aspects of the Eucharist: 1) how the Eucharist is the sacrament of Christ's Body and Blood and of the unity of the Church; 2) the past, present and future meanings of the Eucharist; 3) how it gives us a share in the worship which Christ offers to his Father as our High Priest; and 4) how it gives us a share in the mystery of Christ. For this, I shall draw particularly from what we learn about the Eucharist in the early Church in the catechetical sermons of St Cyril of Jerusalem and St Ambrose, and from the encyclical of Pope John Paul II, *Ecclesia de Eucharistia*.

Remembrance of the Past

Pope John Paul II said that, every time we celebrate Mass, it is as though we put ourselves back at the Last Supper.[240]

---

240. *Ecclesia de Eucharistia* 3.

The Gospels tell us that, at the Last Supper, Christ 'gave thanks' over the bread and cup, and he 'blessed' them. Thus this sacrament is called the Eucharist from the Greek word *eucharistein*, which means to give thanks. In the introductory responses to the Preface before the Eucharistic Prayer, the priest says 'Let us give *thanks* to the Lord our God'. What we give thanks for in the Mass is the saving events by which Christ redeemed us from sin and death: namely, his Passion, resurrection and ascension or, in other words, the Paschal mystery. Thus there is remembering (*anamnesis*) in the Mass of the Paschal Mystery, just as Christ said over the cup, 'Do this in remembrance of me' (Mt 26:26-27). St Paul told the Corinthians that, as often as they eat Christ's body and drink his blood, they recall Christ's death until he comes again (1 Cor 11:26). Thus the Eucharist has a past and a future significance: we look backwards in thanksgiving and forwards in hope. Indeed, in the Mass we look forward precisely by looking back: 'you proclaim his death until he comes again'. The *anamnesis*, or recalling of a past saving event, occurs in the Mass just after the consecration, when we call to mind Christ's Passion, resurrection and ascension.

We learn from the Catechism the following points about remembering past events in the liturgy. First, 'the Christian liturgy not only recalls the events that saved us but actualises, makes them present'.[241] This is particularly true in the Mass, which re-presents, or makes present again, the sacrifice of the Cross. Secondly, it is the Holy Spirit who, 'by his transforming power, makes the mystery

---

241. CCC 1104.

of Christ present here and now'.[242] The Catechism calls the Holy Spirit 'the memory of the Church', because he reminds us of all that Christ said (Jn 14:26). Thirdly, the sacraments 'signify and make actively present the salvation wrought by Christ' and prefigure and anticipate the glory of heaven.[243] A sacrament recalls a past saving event and contains a promise of glory. Thus the Eucharist is 'a pledge of future glory', because by receiving Christ's glorified body and sharing in his risen life, we hope that our bodies too will be raised up again. St Irenaeus thought that sharing in the incorruptible flesh of Christ in the Eucharist helps to make our bodies incorruptible on the Last Day.[244] Christ, in his Discourse on the Bread of Life in John chapter 6, more than once links the Eucharist with our future resurrection: 'Anyone who eats my flesh and drinks my blood has eternal life, and I shall raise him up on the last day' (Jn 6:56). To give another example, St Thomas Aquinas says that the white garment laid on the candidate after the anointing with chrism at baptism is a symbol of the glory of the resurrection.[245]

We recall Christ's passion and death in Mass, because at Mass we do just what he did at the Last Supper, which was to act out symbolically in advance what he was to do the next day by giving up his body and pouring out his blood for us on the Cross, as a sacrifice for the forgiveness of sins. Thus every Mass takes us back to the Last Supper, because we re-enact in it just what Christ did at the Last Supper

---

242. CCC 1092.
243. CCC 1152.
244. *Adversus Haereses* IV 18, 5.
245. ST 3a 66, 10 ad 3.

and commanded the Apostles to do in remembrance of him. We also recall his resurrection, because Christ could not now give us his *life-giving* body and blood unless his body, which suffered death on the Cross, has been raised up to life again. The Mass is, thirdly, a remembering of his ascension, because it is the same body which is present on the altars everywhere beneath the appearances of bread and wine as is seated at the right hand of the Father. Christ is seated in his glorified body at the right hand of the Father as a result of his ascension into heaven, when he withdrew his body in its visible appearance form his disciples on earth. He left us the sacrament of the Eucharist as the means by which his body continues to be present to us, hidden beneath the sacramental appearances of bread and wine. By his ascension, Jesus opened up for us 'the new and living way' through the veil of his flesh into the heavenly sanctuary where he, as our High Priest, continues to plead for us by presenting to his Father the body which he sacrificed on the Cross and the Father glorified at his resurrection and ascension.[246] As the high priests of the Old Testament entered through the curtain of the Temple into the Holy of Holies once a year to offer sacrifice for the atonement of sins, so our way into the heavenly sanctuary is through the veil of Christ's flesh. The Mass also recalls the ascension, because it is a participation on earth in the heavenly liturgy, which our great High Priest offers in the heavenly sanctuary that he entered by his ascension.

As the late Fr Edward Yarnold S.J. points out, to remember in the liturgy is to make Christ's saving events

---

246. Cf. Hebr 10:20.

effective for us.[247] Thus we receive the fruits of Christ's redemption through the Eucharist: these fruits are the forgiveness of sins. As God first redeemed his people, who were slaves in Egypt, by the Passover at the Exodus, when the Hebrew people had to put the blood of a sacrificed lamb on the doors of their houses, so we are now redeemed by the precious blood of the Lamb of God (1 Pet 1:19). Just as the Hebrews ate the lamb which they sacrificed at the Passover meal, so communion is linked with sacrifice in the Eucharist. In the Mass we recall Christ's Passover, which took place within the feast of Passover that recalled the first Passover, when God redeemed his people from Egypt. Thus we see that the Paschal Mystery has its roots in the Old Testament. The Catechism says that the mystery of Christ is hidden in the Old Testament and includes events like the Exodus, the manna, or bread which fell from heaven, and the water which flowed from the rock struck by Moses.[248] St Paul tells us the rock was Christ (1 Cor 10:4). The Mass is the Christian Passover, which Christ initiated at the Last Supper by transforming the Passover that recalled God's act of redemption of the first Passover at the Exodus. Thus the Mass is rooted in the saving history of Israel, which reached its highest point in Christ's death and resurrection.

The Church's Worship

As we have already noted, the Mass is especially the worship of the Church, and this is for two reasons. First,

---

247. *The Awe-inspiring Rites of Initiation*, p.47.
248. CCC 1094.

all the other sacraments are directed to the Eucharist as their goal, the reception of Christ's Body and Blood, which is the source of all the Church's life and the goal of all her activity. Secondly, in the Mass we offer the same sacrifice which Christ offered to his Father on the Cross. All religion in the ancient world included sacrifice, offered to make peace with the gods or God for sins which pagans and Jews alike thought displeased the gods or God. Christ's sacrifice of himself on the Cross is the perfect worship of God, because in this case our High Priest did not offer external things, like animals, but himself, his whole life to God, and, secondly, this offering was a perfect one because it was sinless, as Christ was without sin (Hebr 4:15). Thus, after Christ, it is not possible to offer any better sacrifice than that of Christ, and the Mass remains the one sacrifice to be offered to God, because in it we offer the same sacrifice as Christ did on the Cross. The Mass is, therefore, indeed 'worship in spirit and in truth' (Jn 4:24).

The Eucharist was a sacrifice for St Cyril of Jerusalem and St Ambrose. St Cyril called it 'a spiritual sacrifice'.[249] It is a spiritual sacrifice because, although it is the same sacrifice as Christ offered on the cross, it is offered *in another mode*, as the Council of Trent said; not in a bloody way, as on the Cross, but in an unbloody way.[250] It is also a spiritual sacrifice because the participants offer their worship in a spiritual way with their hearts and minds lifted up to God. St Augustine said that, in offering the sacrifice of the Church, we are to make an altar of our

---

249. *Mystagogical Catecheses* 5, 8.
250. ND 1548.

heart, on which to offer Christ.[251] St Ambrose called the Eucharist an 'oblation'.[252] He was the first to say that the principal person who offers the sacrifice of the Mass is Christ, our High Priest: 'indeed he himself is shown to offer among us, whose word sanctifies the sacrifice which is offered'.[253] The Eucharist is a sacrifice, because it contains in a sacramental way the Blood of Christ, which he poured out for the forgiveness of our sins.

But the Mass is the *same* sacrifice as Christ offered on the Cross. Thus we do not add to Christ's sacrifice, as though it were not perfect and sufficient in itself; nor does the Mass take away from the uniqueness of Christ's sacrifice, which was once-for-all (Hebr 7:27). But the Mass can only be a sacrifice and the same sacrifice if what we offer in it after the consecration is the same as what Christ offered on the Cross, namely, his Body and Blood. Thus the sacrifice of the Mass depends on the Real Presence of Christ's Body and Blood in the Eucharist. We should thus now say a little about the Real Presence, but I would first like to note that the real offering of the Mass does not occur at the part called the Offertory but immediately after the consecration, when it says in all the Eucharistic Prayers of the Roman Missal that we offer Christ's Body and Blood, and (except in Eucharistic Prayer II) this is a sacrifice. The Protestant Reformers in the sixteenth century did not fail to see that the sacrifice of the Mass depends on the Real Presence; so when they

---

251. Augustine, *City of God* X c.3.
252. *De Sacramentis* IV 5, 21.
253. *Enarratio in Ps* 38, 25 (PL 14, 1102).

denied the Catholic doctrine of the Real Presence, they also rejected the Mass as a sacrifice. Thus the Eucharist became just a memorial and communion for them. In recent ecumenical dialogue, however, through taking up the biblical notion of *anamnesis*, there has been a renewed appreciation of the Eucharist as a sacrifice among non-Catholic Christians.

The Reality of the Sacrament

In chapter 8 of Part I, we talked about the 'sacrament alone', 'the reality and sacrament', and the 'reality alone' of each sacrament. The sacrament alone of the Eucharist is the material elements of bread and wine used in it. First, Christ used bread because he wanted his body to be our spiritual food, and wine because this symbolises his precious blood, which he poured out for us. But these elements also signify the unity of the Church, which consists of many members, just as bread is made of many grains and wine out of the juice of many grapes pressed together. Properly speaking, the signs of this sacrament are not bread and wine, for these cease to exist as such after they have been changed into Christ's Body and Blood at the consecration, but the *appearances* of bread and wine, which remain. We distinguish between the appearances of a thing and its substance, what it is.

Speaking to new converts, St Ambrose explained the change of bread and wine in the Eucharist by saying that God who called everything into being out of nothing has the power to change the being, or substance, of something (which he created in the first place) into some new thing.[254] He does this through the power of

---

254. *De Sacramentis* IV 4, 15.

the words spoken at the consecration, which are *Christ's* words, spoken by Christ's priest acting in the person of Christ. These words have creative power to change bread and wine into Christ's Body and Blood, because Christ is the Word of God, by whom all things were made (Jn 1:3). For St Ambrose, the change of bread and wine is effected by the words of consecration, as they are the Words of Christ, who is also God.

> You perhaps say: "My bread is usual". But that bread is bread before the words of the sacraments; when the consecration has been added, from bread it becomes the flesh of Christ… Thus the expression of Christ brings about this sacrament. What is the expression of Christ? Surely that by which all things were made.[255]

It is because of a change of the *being* of bread and wine, in other words of their substance, at the consecration that we speak of 'transubstantiation' (a change of substance). Thus Christ's Body and Blood are *hidden* beneath the outward appearances of bread and wine, not perceptible to sight but only to faith.

While the Church in the West has mainly attributed the change of the bread and wine to the power of the words of consecration, in the East St John Damascene (d. 749) more successfully showed how the change occurs as a result of the creative power of Christ's words *and* the invocation of the Holy Spirit, which immediately precedes the consecration, working together. Like St Ambrose, St John Damascene notes that the words of the Word who made all things can change the things he has made: 'If

---

255. *De Sacramentis* IV 4, 14.

then, the Word of the Lord is living and effectual ... and if by the Word of the Lord the heavens were established ... then can He not make the bread his body and the wine and water his blood?'[256] But the bread and wine are also changed by the working of the Holy Spirit, just as Christ's human body was made when Mary was overshadowed by the Holy Spirit at the Annunciation. St John Damascene also thought that Christ's flesh is life-giving for us, because it was conceived by the Holy Spirit.[257] Another reason why Christ's flesh is life-giving, we may add, is because his body was raised up to life again by the Holy Spirit (Rom 8:11).

The Real Presence means that Christ is not present in the Eucharist with, or beside, bread and wine, but that bread and wine have been changed in their substance into his Body and Blood, because something can only *really* be one thing at a time. The Eucharist cannot *really* be bread and wine *and* the Body and Blood of Christ together. It can only *really* be bread and wine *or* the Body and Blood of Christ. If bread and wine are still present, the Eucharist cannot be *really* the Body and Blood of Christ. If it is the Body and Blood of Christ, then bread and wine have been substantially *changed*. Cardinal Ratzinger (now Pope Benedict XVI) made the same point, that Christ is not present beside or in bread and wine in the Eucharist but bread and wine are changed. He says a 'real transformation' of bread and wine takes place at the consecration, as a result of which something new is there, on the altar, which was not there before. Thus it cannot be that the Body of

256. *De Fide Orthodoxa* IV, c.13 (*The Fathers of the Church* (New York 1958) vol. 37, p.356).
257. Ibid., IV, c.13.

Christ adds itself to bread, as though bread and Christ's Body could exist as two 'substances' side by side.[258] In this way, Ratzinger shows why the Church speaks of a change of substance in the Eucharist, of the substance of bread into the Body of Christ, and of the substance of wine into his blood. As the Council of Trent said, the bread and wine used in the Eucharist become the Body and Blood of Christ 'by a wonderful change' (*mira conversione*).[259]

In agreement with St Ambrose, St Cyril of Jerusalem, says that we have no need to doubt Christ's words, 'This is My Body', 'This is my Blood'. We have no need to doubt the words of Christ, because they are the words of the *Truth* himself. 'He once turned water into wine, in Cana of Galilee, at his own will, and is it incredible that he should have turned wine into blood?'[260]

> Therefore with fullest assurance let us partake as of the Body and Blood of Christ: for in the figure of bread is given to you his Body, and in the figure of wine his Blood; that by partaking of the Body and Blood of Christ, you might be made of the same body and blood with him.[261]

In other words, by receiving Christ's true Body and Blood we are made into his mystical Body, the Church. These are, respectively, the reality and sacrament and the reality alone of the Eucharist.

We have already noted in Part I, chapter 8, some count the true Body and Blood of Christ as the reality and sacrament, while others say this is the unity of the Church,

258. *Christ is Near Us* (San Francisco, Ignatius Press 2003), pp.85-86.
259. *Session* XIII, canon 2 (HD 1527).
260. *Mystagogical Catecheses* 4, 2.
261. Ibid., 4, 3.

because the *res et sacramentum* is how the sacrament relates one to the Church. In favour of the first view, which is the traditional one, it should be said that we become the mystical body of Christ by sharing in his real Body and Blood. The Eucharist, however, is not the sign of the unity of the Church just by her members being joined to one another by communion but they are all joined to one another because each one is first joined to *one* person, Christ. What makes the unity of the Church is the union of each person to one and the same person, Christ. Thus the unity of the Church flows from the interior effect of this sacrament, which is charity. The Eucharist is the sacrament of charity, as baptism is of faith. The Body and Blood of Christ are also the reality and sacrament of the Eucharist, because they are the objective reality of the Eucharist, which exists after the consecration even before anyone has received the sacrament.

The Church is united with Christ through the Eucharist. Colman O'Neill notes that the faithful form the body of Christ because they eat his body.[262] This is another way of putting Augustine's thought that by eating the Body of Christ we become his body, the Church. Père Durrwell quotes St John Chrysostom, who said that the Church is only the body of Christ, because he gives her his body (in the Eucharist), thereby making many into one.[263] Durrwell expresses the relation of the Church to Christ thus: the Church is the body of Christ, because she is united, in all her believers, to the risen body of her saviour.

---

262. Op. cit., p.81.
263. *In Matt. hom.* 82, in Durrwell, *The Resurrection* p. 174.

The Life of the Church

For the remaining part of this chapter on the Eucharist, I shall simply draw attention to some points in Pope John Paul II's encyclical, *Ecclesia de Eucharistia* (The Church draws her life from the Eucharist), which he published on Holy Thursday, 2003. These points illustrate many aspects of the doctrine of the Eucharist. John Paul II called the Eucharist 'the most precious possession of the Church' (paragraph 9), and 'the culmination of all the sacraments' because it perfects our communion with God (34). Through the Eucharist, Christ is always with us, just as he promised the Apostles when he ascended into heaven (1). John Paul II encouraged the faithful to fix their gaze on the Blessed Sacrament, because it is the source and end of the Church's life. In his encyclical for the new millennium, *Novo Millennio Ineunte*, he had already exhorted us to *contemplate the face of Christ*. In his encyclical on the Eucharist, he says that we contemplate the face of Christ in the sacrament of his Body (6). At the same time, we relive in the Eucharist the experience of the two disciples on the road to Emmaus, who recognized Christ in the breaking of bread (6).

The special insight of *Ecclesia de Eucharistia* is that the Eucharist is the *sacrament of the Paschal mystery*. The Church was born from the Paschal mystery, which we commemorate in the Eucharist. This sacrament thus stands at the centre of the Church's life (3). Every time we celebrate Mass, we are taken back to the *Paschal triduum*, the three days from Christ's Passion to his resurrection (4). At the Mass, we return to the hour of the Cross, since it recalls Christ's death. The Mass is 'the sacrifice of the

Cross perpetuated down the ages' (11). The Church's 'foundation and wellspring is the whole *Triduum paschale*', which is recollected in the Eucharist (5).

The central event of our redemption becomes 'really present' in the celebration of the Eucharist, John Paul II says (11). The Mass is inseparably Christ's sacrifice on the Cross, 'made present ever anew', for 'he did not just say "This is my body" but also "given up for you", nor just "This is the cup of my blood" but also "which will be poured out for you".' But there is one single sacrifice: the Mass makes present the sacrifice of the Cross, it does not multiply the sacrifice of Christ (12). What Christ suffered once for all on the Cross was sufficient to take away the sin of the whole world.[264]

Christ does not just give himself to us in communion in the Eucharist but first offers the sacrifice of himself *to the Father*. The Church is also called to offer herself in union with Christ to the Father (13).[265] The Mass not only makes the sacrifice of Christ present again but also his resurrection (14). It reminds us that Christ returned to life for us, since it contains his *life-giving* Body and Blood. As he died on the Cross (the Roman soldiers made sure of this), his body can only be life-giving for us now if it was raised up to life again.

John Paul II reaffirms the teaching of the Council of Trent and of Pope Paul VI in his encyclical, *Mysterium Fidei*, that Christ is really present in the Eucharist. He quotes from the decree on the Eucharist of the Council of

---

264. Cf. CCC 1367, 1382, quoted in *Eccl. de Euch.* 12.
265. Cf. LG 11.

Trent: 'the consecration of the bread effects the change of the whole substance of the bread into the whole substance of the body of Christ our Lord, and of the whole substance of the wine into the substance of his blood'.[266] With Paul VI, he affirms that we must uphold the 'objective reality' of the Eucharist.[267]

After dealing with the sacrifice of the Mass, as part of making the Paschal mystery present again, and with the Real Presence, John Paul II then comes to the effects of receiving the Eucharist on our daily lives. First, he says that the Eucharist 'is intrinsically directed to the inward union of the faithful with Christ through communion' (16). The sacrifice of the Mass and communion are intrinsically related, because we receive the One who sacrificed himself for us. Thus it does not make sense to talk about the Eucharist only as a communion without also teaching about the sacrifice of the Mass, because the whole point about sharing in the Body and Blood of Christ, which are the food and drink in this sacrament, is that they were 'given up for you' and 'poured out for you and for many'. Secondly, since we draw life from the humanity of Christ in the Eucharist, by sharing in his Body and Blood, and his human nature is united to divine nature in Christ, by receiving his Body and Blood we also share in *the life of the Trinity*. As it says in St John: 'As I live because of the Father, so whoever eats me will live because of me' (Jn 6:57). Bl. Columba Marmion makes the point that Christ

---

266. Council of Trent, session XIII c.4: DS 1642. Quoted in CCC 1376.
267. Paul VI, *Solemn Profession of Faith*, 25.

came to give us life (Jn 10:10). He draws life from the Father, and he communicates it to us in the Eucharist. The way he gives us life is by giving himself as food and drink. For Marmion, Christ unites himself with us precisely by being the food of our soul.[268] The Eucharist also gives us a share in the Holy Spirit (17). This is clear in the Third Eucharistic Prayer, in which we pray that 'we, who are nourished by his [Christ's] body and blood, may be filled with his Holy Spirit'. St Paul tells us that those who are joined to Christ's body are one spirit with him (1 Cor 6:17). For Scheeben, we receive the Spirit through the Eucharist, because we receive the flesh of Christ that was conceived, anointed and glorified (raised up) by the Holy Spirit.[269] Thirdly, the Eucharist gives us a pledge of the final resurrection of our body, because we receive Christ's body as it is now, glorified as the result of his resurrection, in the Eucharist (18).

John Paul II next proceeds to show the connection between the Eucharist and the Church in his encyclical. He says that the Church is built up by the sacramental communion of her members (21). She draws strength for her mission in the world by perpetuating the sacrifice of the Cross, which gives courage to all witnesses to Christ (22). Personal union with Christ makes it possible to share in the unity of the Church (23). The Eucharist reinforces one's incorporation into the Church, which was brought about by baptism (22, 23). The Church is also built up by the Adoration of the Blessed Sacrament, which gives

268. *Christ the Life of the Soul*, p.261.
269. *The Mysteries of Christianity*, p.529.

us 'contact with the wellspring of grace' (25). John Paul II reaffirmed that receiving communion presupposes that one already belongs to the communion of the Church (35). He drew a distinction between 'visible communion', which is the outward action of receiving communion, and 'invisible communion', which is being in communion with the Trinity by being in a state of grace (36). 'Visible communion' requires 'invisible communion' (one must be in a state of grace to receive communion). One also needs to be in the unity of the Church, professing the same faith with the Bishop of Rome, who is the visible centre of the Church's unity, in order to receive communion (38). In the same way, the Eucharist also needs to be celebrated in communion with the local bishop, who is in communion with the Pope, who is the successor of St Peter (39). Thus the Eucharist creates communion and maintains it (40). It is indeed 'the sacrament of the Church's unity'.

The unity of the Church is brought about by the union of her members with Christ in the Eucharist. One cannot separate communion from the sacrifice of the Mass. But the sacrifice of the Mass depends on the Real Presence, so that it is the same offering as Christ made to his Father on the Cross. These four main aspects of the Eucharist thus all flow one from another, with their spring in the Real Presence, which is the heart of the Eucharist, because it is by the Real Presence that the sacrament of the Eucharist is the true Body and Blood of Christ.

Chapter Five

Penance

After the three sacraments of initiation come the two sacraments of *healing*: these are penance and anointing of the sick. The anointing of the sick is associated with penance, because its rite includes a place for confession and absolution. The purpose of penance is to restore to grace someone who has lost his or her baptismal grace by sin. A special sacrament of forgiveness is needed for this, because one can only die with Christ to sin once in baptism. If one relapses, another sacrament is needed. Baptism is the *first* sacrament of forgiveness, penance the *second* sacrament of forgiveness. Originally, penance was for those who lapsed from the grace of baptism by serious sins. In the early Church these were principally three: apostasy, murder and adultery, and the penitent was formally reconciled with the Church after a time of penance. In practice, however, following the practice of monks in the sixth and seventh centuries of disclosing their thoughts to a spiritual father, the sacrament also came to be frequently used for venial sins, which do not destroy grace but only lessen charity.

Penance is a sacrament of healing as it cures our human nature that is wounded by sin, for sin has the same effect on our spiritual life as illness does on our natural, bodily life, weakening it so that it is not strong to act well and exercise the virtues. As we noted in the first part, Christ often cured people of their illnesses as a sign that their sins were forgiven. The two go together, because illness and death are the consequence of sin. One of the purposes of the anointing of the sick is to restore the sick person to health, and so to taking a full part in the life of the Church again, when threatened by the consequence of sin – death.

What to Call this Sacrament

For a long time, until the 1960s, this sacrament was simply known as 'confession', from the principal act of the penitent. Now, however, it is known by several names, of which the two most general ones are penance and Reconciliation. It is not called penance because the penitent performs a penance to make amendment for his or her sins, but because the word 'penance' comes from the Latin word *paenitentia*, which means repentance. In St Thomas Aquinas' view, this was especially the sacrament of the *virtue of repentance*, which is sorrow about sin. We can have a sacrament of a virtue, because materially this sacrament consists of the acts of the *recipient*, who is the penitent. As St Thomas says, this virtue is sorrow about sin with the intention of removing it.[270] This virtue is essential to the sacrament, because God cannot forgive any sin unless there is sorrow for sin in the sinner. This is because he respects our free will and does not force it to bend back. Nonetheless, God instils this virtue in us by turning our heart back to him: as it says 'Convert us, O Lord, and we will be converted to you' (Lam 5:21). Thus the virtue of repentance goes with conversion, which is

---

270. ST 3a 85, 1.

literally a turning towards God by a change of heart.

This sacrament is also commonly called that of Reconciliation, because the reality and sacrament are that the sinner is reconciled with God and with the Church. One reason why we have a special sacrament of forgiveness is that the sinner is reconciled with God *by being reconciled with the Church*. We easily forget today why the first converts to Christianity wanted to be baptised, and so join the Church, on the day of Pentecost, which was *so that they could have their sins forgiven*, when they heard St Peter appeal to them: 'Repent and be baptised everyone of you in the name of Jesus Christ *for the forgiveness of your sins*' (Acts 2:38).

Perhaps the best name for this sacrament is the sacrament of Mercy, which puts the emphasis on God's part, the source of forgiveness. We have a special sacrament of mercy because, as St Paul said, the mercy of God appeared visibly in Christ Jesus (Tit 2:11; 3:6). This was by the mystery of the incarnation.

Mercy and Forgiveness in Scripture

The evidence for this sacrament in the New Testament is clear. First, when Christ told St Peter that he is the rock on which he will build his Church, he immediately added: 'I will give you the keys of the kingdom of heaven, and whatever you bind on earth shall be bound in heaven, and whatever you loose on earth shall be loosed in heaven' (Mt 16:19). The power of binding and loosing sins is part of the Apostolic ministry, which Christ entrusted to the Apostles, and they and their successors, the bishops, hand on by the sacrament of ordination. We see how this power can be given to men in the cure of the paralytic (Mark 2:1-11). When Jesus told the paralytic 'My son, your sins are forgiven', the people around him were shocked and rightly objected, 'Who can forgive sins but God alone?' Then Jesus replied, 'But that you may know that the Son of man has authority on earth to forgive sins', and told the paralytic to get up. He thereby implied that he, the Son of man, was also God and indicated that God could forgive sins through the ministry of human agents, which is why we have a *sacrament* of forgiveness. This is possible through the incarnation because God became man. Properly speaking, only God forgives sins: the priest *absolves* the penitent from sin. The absolution spoken by the priest is the *sacramental sign* that God has forgiven the sinner. The Son of man's authority to forgive sin was part of his authority, which he received from his Father and passed on to the Apostles at his ascension: 'All authority in heaven and on earth has been given to me' (Mt 28:18).

A second passage about binding and loosing occurs in St Matthew 18:15-18. The new dimension here is that the community or the Church is involved in the forgiveness of sins. Significantly, Matthew 16:18 and 18:17 are the only two passages in the four Gospels, which use the word *ekklesia*. Matthew chapter 18 shows that the correction of sinners was the care of the whole community in the early Church. When a brother failed to heed a first call to correction, he was to be taken before the church. Correction involved two or three witnesses after the first warning, and the community after the second warning. This practice shows how the forgiveness of sin was connected to reconciliation with the Church from the beginning. In a large fresco about the Church in the Spanish chapel of Santa Maria Novella in Florence, the path up to heaven is marked by Dominican friars seated at the roadside, hearing confessions, who thus lead souls to salvation by loosing their sins.

In the Gospel of St John, Jesus gives power to loose sins to the Apostles when he breathes the Holy Spirit on them on the day that he rose from the dead, saying: 'Receive the Holy Spirit. If you forgive the sins of any, they are forgiven; if you retain the sins of any, they are retained' (Jn 20:23). The connection of the forgiveness of sins with the Holy Spirit is now reflected in the prayer before absolution in the new rite of penance: 'and has sent the Holy Spirit among us for the forgiveness of sins'. Our sins are forgiven by the Holy Spirit, just as Jesus cast out demons by the Holy Spirit (Mt 12:28).

The mercy of God, which the sacrament of penance signifies, is perhaps best illustrated by the parable of the Prodigal Son in St Luke, chapter 15. Here it will be sufficient to note just a few points in this parable for our purposes. First, the younger son leaves his father and wanders to a distant country. This is an image of sin, which St Augustine called 'the region of unlikeness' (*dissimilitudo*), as sin impairs the image of God in us. Secondly, after a change of heart, literally 'having gone into himself' (15:17), as though we leave our true selves when we abandon God, the son is restored straightaway to his original position in the house of his father. The father does not make him first serve in an inferior position but treats him as an equal with the elder son who had remained at home, by putting a ring on his finger and ordering a feast for the son who returned. This illustrates the effect of the sacrament, which restores the sinner to his or her former grace, as will be discussed more fully below. Thirdly, the parable implies that having one's sins forgiven is a kind of resurrection, for the two halves of the parable end with the same refrain: 'for this son was dead, and is alive again; he was lost, and is found' (Lk 15:24, 32). The Catechism calls the forgiveness of sins a 'spiritual resurrection'.[271] G. K. Chesterton said that one is remade in the image of God by confession: 'he walks out into the dawn of a new day'.[272]

The parable of the Prodigal Son follows two other parables about finding the lost sinner in Luke, chapter 15. The first of these is about the shepherd who leaves the ninety-nine 'righteous' sheep in order to seek the one lost sheep. The Catechism remarks that Christ shows himself to be the Good Shepherd by forgiving sinners. When a priest administers the sacrament of penance (or Mercy), he fulfils the ministry of the Good Shepherd who seeks the lost sheep.[273] The priest is the sign and instrument of God's merciful love for the sinner. In confession, we encounter Christ, represented by his priest, especially as the Good Shepherd. Pope John Paul II even said in his first encyclical, *Redemptor Hominis*, that Christ has a right to meet us in confession.[274]

---

271. CCC 1468.
272. *Autobiography* (London 1937) p.329.
273. CCC 1465.
274. *Redemptor hominis* 20, 6.

The Structure of the Sacrament

The sacrament of penance is brought about by the active co-operation of the recipient with the minister, unlike some sacraments, in which the minister alone makes the sacrament. The acts of the penitent include *repentance, confession,* and *satisfaction*. The penitent makes satisfaction by carrying out the 'penance' assigned by the confessor. The act of the minister is the prayer of absolution. The acts of the penitent are regarded in theology as the *matter* of the sacrament, and the words of absolution as the *form*, for the sins that are confessed provide what is to be forgiven and taken away in this sacrament. The words of absolution make the repentance and confession of sins by the penitent be the sacrament of forgiveness. The penitent needs to have sorrow for sin if the absolution spoken by the priest is to be effective. The sacraments are not automatic: if they are to be effective, they need to be received with a suitable disposition. Usually this disposition is a state of grace and charity, but when the sacrament is for putting one back into a state of grace, it requires repentance, because God does not forcibly remove our sins against our will but waits for us to turn back to him. Thus forgiveness goes with a conversion of heart. Aquinas says that the first act of repentance is contrition. Of course contrition itself is marked with charity, which is the love of God, as we shall see later.

Aquinas says that contrition is the immediate effect, and so the *res et sacramentum* of this sacrament, because the visible acts of the penitent are the sign of inner sorrow.[275] The *res tantum* (interior grace) for Aquinas is,

---

275. ST 3a 84, 1 ad 3.

then, the forgiveness of sin, which is the interior effect in the recipient. Some writers, like Vorgrimler, count reconciliation with the Church as the *res et sacramentum* (mystery of the Church), and reconciliation with God as the *res tantum* (interior effect). But Colman O'Neill thought that this misinterprets Aquinas' teaching about the justification of the sinner and the sacrament as a cause of grace. Although grace is needed for contrition, for God first moves the heart to repentance, grace is given through the sacrament, which consists in the acts of the penitent (plus absolution). The sinner is justified by the forgiveness of his sins, but there is no forgiveness without repentance, which is a free act. God draws back the sinner to himself by his mercy, but he does this in a way that respects the free will of the sinner, so that repentance is an act of free will. Thus, for O'Neill, contrition is the intermediate effect of the sacrament (*res et sacramentum*), and reconciliation the final effect (*res tantum*).[276] He supports this view by saying that reconciliation cannot be the *res et sacramentum* of penance, because there is no question of reconciliation with the Church when only venial sins are confessed.[277]

The confession of sins to a minister of the Church is integral to the conversion of the sinner. As St Jerome remarked: How can the doctor cure the patient unless he shows his wound? By confessing his sins, the penitent shows that he has a contrite heart, which has withdrawn from sin. The absolution spoken by the priest is the sign that God remits the sin. Contrition goes with repentance. Haffner

276. *Meeting Christ in the Sacraments*, p.263.
277. Ibid., p.266.

says that contrition means the crushing of sin.[278] This, however, seems wrong: contrition is rather the crushing of the heart that is smitten by sorrow for sin, as the Psalmist speaks of 'a humble and contrite heart' (Ps 50:17).

There are two kinds of contrition: imperfect and perfect. Imperfect contrition is also known as attrition. The difference between the two is that imperfect contrition arises from the fear of punishment, and perfect contrition is the sorrow for sin which arises from the love of God. St John says 'Love casts out fear' (1 Jn 4:18). Contrition does not depend on the *feeling* of sorrow: the objective criterion of contrition is rather the resolve not to commit sin again. There is no contrition without the gift of grace. Colman O'Neill defines contrition as 'sorrow for sin inspired by charity'.[279] The Council of Trent described the process of conversion with psychological insight thus:

> But that imperfect contrition, which is called attrition, … if it excludes the will of sinning with the hope of pardon, not only declares that a man is not made a hypocrite and so the more a sinner, but also that it is a gift of God and impulse of the Holy Spirit, who admittedly does not dwell in the sinner but only moves him, by which the person is helped to prepare the way back to justice.[280]

The decree of Trent here speaks of someone who has lost all grace, not of someone who only has venial sins. We notice in this description that the initiative comes from the grace of God. The sinner is also justified, made just again, by

---

278. *The Sacramental Mystery*, p.130.
279. Op. cit., p.261.
280. Session 14, c.4 (DS 1678, ND 1624).

this sacrament, just as he or she was first justified by the sacrament of baptism. The justification of the sinner is an effect of Christ's redemptive death on the cross, by which he atoned for sin. To be justified means that the right order between the human person and God is restored. To offend God by going against his Will breaks the order of justice, or uprightness, in which God first established the parents of the human race. When God justifies us he not only forgives our sin, so that he no longer counts it against us, but he also renews our nature with a positive gift of grace.[281] This is another reason why, in order to have our sins forgiven, it is not enough to repent within oneself, but it is also necessary to turn to the visible body of the Church, because we are not justified by faith alone but also by the sacraments of the Church, which apply the Passion of Christ to the individual.

Thus repentance is more than sorrow for sin: it includes the readiness to make reparation for sin, so that the order of justice is restored. The Catechism says that the meaning of doing a penance is that it signifies a willingness to accept the cross of Christ.[282] Thirty years earlier, Colman O'Neill had written that, as the only adequate satisfaction for sin is the Passion of Christ, we need to accept Christ's atoning death with faith.[283] We accept Christ as the expiation for our sins, when we approach the sacraments, which apply his Passion to the individual. Doing the penance given in confession is a sign of the penitent's willingness to share

---

281. See Part 1, chapter 7 on justification as an effect of all the sacraments.
282. CCC 1460.
283. *Meeting Christ in the Sacraments*, p.264. Cf. Rom 3:25.

in Christ's Passion in some small way. St Thomas says that the Passion of Christ works in the sacrament of penance through the absolution of the priest simultaneously with the work of the penitent, who co-operates with grace for the destruction of sin.[284]

The Effects of the Sacrament of Penance

The effects of this sacrament may be listed as follows: 1) forgiveness of sins, 2) restoration to grace, 3) reconciliation with the Church and with God, and 4) a spiritual resurrection by which the sinner passes 'from death to life' even in the present life.[285]

1. God totally forgives all sins that are confessed, although the effect of sin, which weakens the will, may still remain in the sinner. It is as though God buries our sins at the bottom of the sea, having tied them to a millstone (Mic 7:19).

2. The effect of forgiveness is that someone is restored to his or her former state of grace and, if there was a total lapse of grace, all the good one had done before is living with charity once again. As there is no remission of sin without an infusion of grace, all the virtues previously possessed by the penitent return with this grace, although some effects of sin may remain as a tendency which makes it more difficult for the sinner to exercise these virtues; but this difficulty may be overcome by the inclination of charity given with grace.[286] Does the repentant sinner have more or less virtue after rising again from sin? St Thomas says that, as the disposition for grace depends on the movement of free will, it depends

---

284. ST 3a 84, 5.
285. For spiritual resurrection, CCC 1470. Cf. Jn 5:24.
286. ST 3a 89, 1 ad 3.

on the firmness of free will, so that someone may rise to a greater degree of virtue than before; but sometimes it is to the same degree and sometimes to a lesser one.[287] It is possible to rise to a higher state of virtue, because the penitent may have become more humble as a result of falling. Good works, which become dead and of no use for leading to eternal salvation through mortal sin, become living and meritorious again after a return to grace, because God accepts them.[288] When sin is remitted through the sacrament, the guilt of sin, which is an obstacle to entering heaven, is taken away, but absolution does not remove the disorders of fallen nature, so one still suffers temptation.

3. The Catechism names *reconciliation with God* as 'the purpose and effect of this sacrament'.[289] It also teaches that the reconciliation with God goes inseparably with reconciliation with the Church.[290] This is because the power of binding and loosing was entrusted to the Church through the Apostolic ministry: whatever is loosed on earth is loosed in heaven. Reconciliation with the Church is, therefore, the path to entering heaven. We are also reconciled with God by being reconciled with the Church, because God has reconciled us with himself *through Christ*: 'It was God who reconciled us to himself through Christ and gave us the work of handing on this reconciliation', St Paul says (2 Cor 5:18). As reconciliation is through Christ, it is through his body, the Church. The ministry of reconciliation is given to the ministers of the

---

287. ST 3a 89, 2.
288. ST 3a 89, 5.
289. CCC 1468.
290. CCC 1445.

Church just as it was given to St Paul, who saw himself as 'an ambassador of Christ', appealing to the Corinthians to be reconciled with God (2 Cor 5:20). To repent and be forgiven is to be reconciled with God.

Two further effects follow through this sacrament, which is the *sign* of reconciliation with God: peace and friendship with God. Peace with God comes from the peace which Christ made by the cross: 'so making peace, that he might reconcile both (Jews and Gentiles) to God in one body through the cross' (Eph 2:17; Col 1:20). Christ made peace when he destroyed sin by his death on the cross. The Venerable Cardinal Newman thought that, after the Eucharist, this sacrament was the most heavenly because of the peace it brings to the penitent.[291] We need this sacrament, because no one can speak peace to himself but someone else, in this case a priest representing Christ and the Church, can speak it to us.

The second effect of reconciliation is that we are restored to friendship with God, as the Catechism says when it names the effects of this sacrament, 'of which the most precious is friendship with God'.[292] St Thomas too implies that confession is a reconciliation in friendship when he says that the debt of blame is contrary to friendship.[293] Therefore, to have this debt forgiven is to be restored to friendship. We have friendship with God because of the Holy Spirit, who is the Love of God. As the forgiveness of sins is through the Holy Spirit, who is the Love of God, so

---

291. *The Present Position of Catholics in England*, (Longmans, Green & Co. 1985) p.351.
292. CCC 1468.
293. ST 3a, 86, 3 ad 4.

he makes us friends of God. This is implied in the prayer before absolution in the revised rite of penance: 'and has sent the Holy Spirit among us for the forgiveness of sins'. Sin affects or breaks friendship with God.

4. God reconciles the world to himself not only by the death of his Son but also by his *resurrection* because, as the Council of Trent noted, Christ instituted this sacrament principally when, after his resurrection, he breathed upon his disciples and said 'Receive the Holy Spirit. If you forgive the sins of any, they are forgiven; if you retain the sins of any, they are retained' (Jn 20:22-23).[294] As already noted, the sacrament works a spiritual resurrection, because the penitent rises from sin to grace again. This too is expressed in the prayer before absolution: 'God, the Father of mercies, has reconciled the world to himself, by the death and resurrection of his Son'.

Besides these effects, we may name some others. Pope John Paul II, in an address to the Apostolic Penitentiary in Rome, March 2002, said that this sacrament increases grace, strengthens virtue, and helps to weaken tendencies to sin. Fr Paul Haffner names as effects the threefold reconciliation noted by John Paul II in his Apostolic Exhortation *Reconciliatio et Paenitentia* 31, V: reconciliation with oneself, with one's brothers and sisters, and with God.

Why We need a Sacrament of Forgiveness

It is difficult for people who are not Catholics to see why

---

294. Session XIV c.1 (ND 1617). See also Trent sess. VI c.14 (ND 1943).

one needs to confess one's sins to a priest to have them forgiven. Why is it not enough to say 'sorry' to God in one's heart alone? Some of the reasons in answer to this question have already been given. We are justified by the sacraments; we cannot be healed without telling the doctor what is wrong with us (Christ is the divine Physician of souls whom we meet in this sacrament); forgiveness is not just a matter of saying 'sorry' to God but we need to put sin right by penance. Strictly speaking, the sacrament of penance is only necessary for salvation in the case of a total lapse from grace after baptism by mortal sin. But in the practice and tradition of the Church, it has come to be used regularly as a means of preserving and increasing spiritual health, not least because it helps one to grow in humility, the foundation of the virtues. Nor should we forget that receiving the Eucharist is another means of obtaining forgiveness of sins, but the Eucharist only takes away daily, venial sins by an increase of charity. The Eucharist cannot restore one to grace, which one needs for receiving communion, when this has been altogether lost. For this we need the sacrament of penance (*paenitentia*, repentance).

As already said, we need the sacrament of penance, because we are reconciled to God by being reconciled with the Church. As the Church is a visible body, so we are reconciled with her by a visible sign. We are also reconciled with the Church formally and visibly by a special sacrament, because sin harms the Church as well as the individual. This is because the lessening of charity in one person means that much less charity is in the Church. Less charity in me affects my relation to others around me. St Paul saw that, if one member of the body suffers, the whole body suffers (1 Cor 12:26). As the Catechism says, sin 'damages communion with the Church. For this reason conversion entails both God's forgiveness and reconciliation with the Church.'[295] We are reconciled with God through a sacrament because, as Pope John Paul II said, 'The mission of reconciliation is proper to the whole Church.'[296] The Second Vatican Council made us aware again of the dimension of the Church in the sacrament of penance, which had become the most private of sacraments. It called for baptism and penance to be given greater emphasis in the liturgy and catechesis during Lent as a means of preparing the faithful for Easter.[297] The liturgy of Eastertide also frequently reminds us of the forgiveness of sins, as the new members of the Church had had all their sins forgiven by baptism at the Easter Vigil. Forgiveness is an effect of the resurrection, for we are baptised into the death and resurrection of Christ. As it says in the sequence for Mass in Easter week (*Victimae paschali*):

> The lamb has redeemed the sheep. Christ, the innocent One, has reconciled sinners with God. Christ has redeemed the world by his death and resurrection together.

Colman O'Neill sees the following reasons for linking the forgiveness of sins with a special sacrament. First, faith alone is not enough for sharing in the life of the body of the Church. As we are corporeal creatures, our life with others in the Church must also be expressed and nourished by

---

295. CCC 1440.
296. *Reconciliatio et Paenitentia* 12.
297. SC 109.

bodily signs of grace.[298] This sacrament also corresponds to a human need to receive an assurance of forgiveness and inner peace from others. The advantages of receiving this sacrament are that it gives us security and peace, because it frees us from any lingering doubt about whether our sin has been forgiven by God. As sin turns us inwards to ourselves, so the act of confessing to another person helps us to overcome sin by turning us out of ourselves to others. John Paul II thought that confession is salutary for us, because when a person confesses he comes in touch with the truth about himself, and this puts him in touch with God.[299]

In his Apostolic Exhortation *Reconciliation and Penance*, published in 1984, Pope John Paul II said that we meet Christ, who is our brother, in this sacrament. He is our merciful and compassionate High Priest, who was tempted as we are but did not sin (Hebr 4:14-15). We also meet Christ the divine Physician who heals and comforts us.[300] As receiving this sacrament of penance conforms us with Christ in his passion, it also enables us to share more fully in the sacrifice of the Mass and makes us more docile to the promptings of the Holy Spirit.

---

298. *Meeting Christ with the Sacraments,* p.265.

299. *Sign of Contradiction*, p.142

300. *Reconciliatio et Paenitentia* 29.

Chapter Six
The Anointing of the Sick

The anointing of the sick is associated with penance as the second sacrament of healing and because it also contains a place for confession and absolution. It clearly shows that the sacraments are the means by which Christ continues the ministry of healing he performed during his life on earth. As the Catechism remarks, Christ continues his ministry of healing and compassion through the sacraments. Just as Christ let himself be touched by the sick, and touched them himself, so we still have contact with Christ through the sacraments.[301] We would expect Christ to provide a special sacrament of healing, since illness is a condition of physical weakness when we need to be strengthened, and one which can threaten life.

There are clear signs that Christ left us this sacrament in the New Testament. According to St Mark, when the Apostles were sent out on their first mission, 'they cast out many demons, and anointed with oil many that were sick and healed them' (Mk 6:13). Mark alone tells us that one of the things which Jesus told the Eleven that the faithful would do after the resurrection was that they would lay hands on the sick and cure them: 'they will lay their hands on the sick and they will recover' (Mk 16:18). Laying on of hands forms the *epiclesis* in the rite of anointing, which

---

301. CCC 1503. Cf. Mk 1:41; Lk 6:19.

precedes the prayer of blessing over the oil that comes just before the anointing itself. We thus find anointing with oil combined with the laying on of hands in healing the sick in the New Testament. In the well known passage from St James, used as the opening of the rite of the sacrament, it says:

> 'Is anyone among you sick? Let him call for the elders (presbyters) of the Church and let them pray over him, anointing him with oil in the name of the Lord; and the prayer of faith will save the sick man, and the Lord will raise him up; and if he has committed any sins, he will be forgiven' (Jas 5:14-15).

We may notice two points in this passage. First, when the presbyters prayed over the sick person, we may conclude that they also laid hands on him or her. Secondly, the anointing of the sick included the forgiveness of sin, which is part of the meaning of the sacrament. In quoting this passage from St James, the Catechism concludes: 'Tradition has recognized in this rite one of the seven sacraments'.[302] The Council of Trent taught that this sacrament was instituted by Christ, seeing an allusion to it in Mark 6:13. Trent says that it was 'recommended to the faithful and promulgated by James the apostle and brother of the Lord'.[303]

There has been a change of the name of the sacrament, which reflects a change in the understanding of it. Until the 1950s, it was known as 'Extreme Unction' (the last anointing), as though it was especially for someone who

---

302. CCC 1510.
303. Session XIV, *Decree on the Last Anointing,* c.1: (ND 1636).

was '*in extremis*', in danger of death. This means that it was not generally thought to be a sacrament of healing but principally one to help the sick person in the final stage of life, the transition to death. Indeed, when people saw the priest come with the holy oils, they often thought that their end was near. Now, however, the sacrament is no longer called Extreme Unction but the anointing of the sick. This has two results. First, the sacrament is not only for the dying but for anyone who is seriously ill or in a sufficiently frail condition that could lead to death, although this may not seem imminent. This was the wish of the Second Vatican Council: "Extreme Unction" which may also and more fittingly be called "Anointing of the Sick" is not a sacrament intended only for those at the point of death. Hence it is certain that as soon as any of the faithful begins to be in danger of death from sickness or old age, this is already a suitable time for them to receive this sacrament'.[304] The sacrament should, however, be reserved for those who are physically ill rather than just psychologically weak. Secondly, as the words of the 'form' of the sacrament imply, it is not just for strengthening someone for dying well in Christ but also for the recovery of someone's health, so that he or she rises to full life again, as is clear from the essential rite:

> Through this holy anointing may the Lord in his love and mercy help you with the grace of the Holy Spirit. May the Lord who frees you from sin save you and raise you up.

The anointing with oil (on the forehead and hands) is itself a sign of the grace of the Holy Spirit.

---

304. SC 73. Cf. CCC 1514.

The Meaning of Suffering

We can only understand this sacrament if we also reflect on the origin and meaning of suffering and death. From the perspective of Christian faith, illness is a consequence of sin, not necessarily of the actual sin of the individual but of the sin of Adam, which has affected the human nature of everyone descended from him (except Our Lord's human nature and Our Lady). Sin caused the original integration of human nature to be lost: this disintegration is manifest in illness, which eventually leads to the total disintegration of the body in death. The disintegration of death will be finally reversed and overcome by the resurrection of the body, to which we look forward in hope. Christ made plain that not all illness is directly related to the sin of the ill person,[305] or else better people would suffer less. On the contrary, some saints, like St Bernadette and St Thérèse of Lisieux, suffered much and died young. But illness entered as a consequence of sin: it is a sign of our fallen human nature. Although baptism takes away the guilt of original sin, so that it is no longer an obstacle to entering heaven, and restores us to the sonship of God, it does not restore us to immortality, which Adam lost, or to freedom from suffering.[306]

The only true evil is what can separate us eternally from God: this is not illness, suffering, or the evils of injustice, which people suffer in this world, but the guilt of sin. On the contrary, what is seen as evil can become

305. Cf. John 9:3: 'It was not this man who sinned, or his parents'.
306. Cf. C. O'Neill, op. cit., p.276.

a means of uniting us more closely with Christ and lead to conversion. Christ himself, though he was sinless, did not evade suffering and death. Although suffering is an evil in itself, for it would not arise unless human beings committed wrong, God can draw good out of it. Illness can be God's way of drawing us more closely to him, as happened with St Francis of Assisi and St Ignatius of Loyola, who underwent conversion through a time of convalescence following injury in fighting. The Christian can give positive meaning to his or her sufferings by uniting them with Christ's suffering on the Cross. Isaiah reveals, in the Song of the Suffering Servant, that suffering can have a redemptive meaning for the sins of others: 'my servant shall make many to be accounted righteous; and he shall bear their iniquities' (Isa 53:11). St Paul talks about completing 'what is lacking in Christ's afflictions for the sake of his body, which is the Church' through his own sufferings (Col 1:24). Thus this sacrament helps one to associate one's suffering with that of Christ's. As the Catechism says, 'By the grace of this sacrament the sick person receives the strength and the gift of uniting himself more closely to Christ's Passion: in a certain way he is *consecrated* to bear fruit by configuration to the Saviour's redemptive Passion. Suffering, a consequence of original sin, acquires a new meaning: it becomes a participation in the saving work of Jesus'.[307]

As Colman O'Neill says, suffering becomes a means of growing in the likeness of Christ (configuration). This sacrament enables the sick person to be conformed with

---

307. CCC 1521.

Christ by readily accepting his or her suffering and illness. The worship of God in the Church, the perfect example of which is the worship which Christ offered in the sacrifice of himself on the Cross, is advanced by the suffering of her members in union with Christ.[308] Suffering does not just produce in us conformity with Christ's Passion and death but also with his *resurrection*. St Paul expressed the desire 'that I may know him (Christ) and the power of his resurrection, and may share his sufferings, becoming like him in his death, that if possible I may attain the resurrection from the dead' (Phil 3:10-11). The sacrament of anointing of the sick opens up the way to the resurrection by joining the ill person to Christ's passion and death, so that he or she rises again with him.

Thus we have a sacrament for when the powers of a Christian are threatened by illness and suffering, and for protecting his or her virtues, which are often assailed just before death. Some undergo temptations against faith as they perceive the approaching darkness of death. The rite of anointing includes a renewed profession of faith in the Creed. The Catechism remarks that illness can lead to despair and rebellion against God. The anointing of the sick is a sacrament of *hope,* since it gives the ill person confidence in God's love and mercy. It is also a sacrament of hope, because it looks forward to our final rising up at the resurrection of the dead. This sacrament is 'intended to strengthen those who are being tried by illness.'[309] Thus it gives the sick person the grace to bear

---

308. Op. cit., p.282.
309. CCC 1511.

his or her sufferings with *patience,* and it defends and increases the virtue of fortitude, of which patience is a part, in bearing afflictions. This fortitude, Aquinas says, is especially the strength of mind by which one is ready to accept suffering.[310] The Christian is made perfect by accepting suffering in conformity with Christ, who was made perfect by suffering (Hebr 2:10). St Paul help us to see that the fortitude which this sacrament gives comes from Christ when he says: 'I will all the more boast of my weaknesses, that the power of Christ may rest upon me … for when I am weak, then I am strong' (2 Cor 12:9-10).

Colman O'Neill notes that suffering and death are an integral part of human life on the way to glory, just as the Christ first had to suffer and enter into glory (Lk 24:26). We know that the sufferings of this life are winning for us a weight of glory (Rom 8:18). Thus O'Neill connects the anointing of the sick with the *resurrection* of Christ as well as with his death.[311] The resurrection shows us that salvation includes the body as well as the soul. Thus we have a special sacrament for the healing of the body. O'Neill points out that redemption is not just from sin but also from death.[312] Haffner remarks that the sacrament either brings about a healing of the body or, if the sick person is not made well again, it is a preparation for glory. The passage in St James shows that Christ came to redeem the *whole* person: body and soul. The presbyters pray for the sick person's recovery, and his sins are forgiven. Thus the

---

310. Cf. ST 2a 2ae 123, 1.
311. Op. cit., p.274.
312. Ibid., pp.272-273.

sacrament is for the healing of body and soul: for being freed from illness and from sin, which is the source of illness in the human race. The Catechism remarks that Christ's miracles of healing were often done as a sign that the cured person's sin had been forgiven.[313] As Jesus was concerned with healing the whole person, he has left us a sacrament for the restoration of bodily health (anointing) as well as for the healing of the soul (penance).

The Effects of the Sacrament of Anointing

The purpose of this sacrament is to strengthen the Christian in illness. Its principal effect, Colman O'Neill says, is interior healing. The sign of this is anointing with oil, which is applied to wounds and injuries for its soothing properties. In all healing, medicine is applied from without but the healing goes on *within* the person. Christ cured people physically and their sins were forgiven – bodily and spiritual healing occurred together. Thus the Council of Trent said that the anointing of the sick complements the sacrament of penance and the whole Christian life, which should contain an element of penance.[314]

The Council of Trent describes the reality (*res*) and effect of this sacrament with the words of St James: 'the prayer of faith will save the sick person, and the Lord will raise him up; and anyone who has committed sins will be forgiven'.[315] The Council of Trent continued: 'The reality

---

313. CCC 1503. Cf. Mk 2:10; Jn 5:14.
314. Session XIV, *Decree on Last Anointing*, proemium (ND 1635).
315. Ibid., c.2 (ND 1637).

is the grace of the Holy Spirit, whose anointing takes away sins if there still be any to be expiated, and also the remains of sin; it comforts and strengthens the soul of the sick person by awakening in him great confidence in the divine mercy'. Trent recalled here the opinion of St Thomas Aquinas, who listed the remission of sin and its after-effects or remnants (*reliquiae*) as the effect of this sacrament.[316] These are the effects named in the essential words of the rite: 'May the Lord help you with the grace of the Holy Spirit … May the Lord who frees you from sin save you and raise you up'. As already said, the grace of the Holy Spirit is signified by the anointing with oil.

The principal effect, then, is that the sacrament heals the wounds of sin. This is the *res et sacramentum* of this sacrament. But it also includes a prayer for bodily healing. This was already envisaged by the Council of Trent, which said the sacrament is not only for the dying but for the seriously ill.[317] Thus one of the effects of this sacrament is to restore to health, if this is expedient for the salvation of the sick person, for this benefits the life of grace.[318]

The interior effect (*res tantum*) of this sacrament is to unite the sick person with the suffering of Christ, and so conform him or her with the Passion of Christ. As the Second Vatican Council said, this sacrament commends the sick person to the suffering and death of Christ.[319] The Catechism likewise teaches: 'By the grace of this sacrament the sick person receives the strength and the gift of uniting

---

316. ST 3a Supplementum 30, 1.
317. ND 1638.
318. ND 1637.
319. LG 11.3.

himself more closely to Christ's Passion.[320] This is for the good of the person and of the whole Church, for we can thereby make up what is lacking in Christ's sufferings for the sake of his body, the Church (Col 1:24). The sick person is thus enabled to accept his or her suffering and death in conformity with Christ.[321] Another result is inner peace and 'clarity of conscience'.[322]

Viaticum

The anointing of the sick completes our conformity with the death and resurrection of Christ, which began with baptism.[323] As it helps us to accept our death in union with Christ, it also prepares us for heaven and the glory of the resurrection. This sacrament completes our pilgrimage on earth, which has for its goal our heavenly homeland.[324] Thus it is desirable that *viaticum*, which is communion for the last stage of our journey, be given within the rite of anointing. As the Eucharist recalls the Paschal mystery, it is especially appropriate that it be given at the moment of the 'passing over' of the sick person to the heavenly Father. As the Catechism reminds us, the Eucharist is 'the seed of eternal life': 'Whoever eats my flesh and drinks my blood has eternal life, and I will raise him up at the last day' (Jn 6:54). The Catechism says about *viaticum*, 'The Eucharist is here the sacrament of passing over from death to life,

---

320. CCC 1521.
321. C. O'Neill, op. cit., p.292. Cf. CCC 1505.
322. ST 3a Suppl. 29, 4 ad 1.
323. CCC 1523.
324. CCC 1525.

from this world to the Father'.[325] The 'Eucharist should always be the last sacrament of the earthly journey, the "viaticum" for "passing over" to eternal life'.[326] Thus the anointing of the sick is suitably administered within Mass, for the Eucharist is the memorial of Christ's Passover and the goal of all the sacraments. Fr Haffner observes that the sacrament of anointing applies the power of the whole Paschal mystery to us, since it unites us with Christ in his Passion and death and prepares us for the resurrection, which will be the final healing of our body.[327]

Faith Healing

As the prayer of 'faith healers' often seems to have more effect in curing sick people, one may wonder whether there is any special benefit in receiving the sacrament of the anointing of the sick. Is it not better to obtain someone with the charism of healing rather than call for a priest with the holy oils? There is, however, a difference between faith healing and the sacrament. First, to posses the power to heal with faith is a *charism* (1 Cor 12:9). Secondly, only the sacrament forgives sins and produces conformity with Christ in his suffering. Thus the sacrament is quite objective in its effects even when it does not restore the recipient to health, whereas the faith healer achieves much less if he does not heal physically, except for the peace his prayer may bring to the sick person. The effectiveness of faith healing depends on the personal charism of the

---

325. CCC 1524.
326. CCC 1517.
327. *The Sacramental Mystery*, p.145.

healer; the sacrament does not depend on the qualities of the priest but on Christ working through the sacraments, as his instrument, by the power of the Holy Spirit.

The first effect of the sacrament listed in the Catechism is 'a particular gift of the Holy Spirit. The first grace of this sacrament is one of strengthening, peace and courage to overcome the difficulties that go with the condition of serious illness or the frailty of old age. This grace is a gift of the Holy Spirit, who renews faith and trust in God and strengthens against the temptation of the evil one, the temptation to discouragement in the face of death'.[328] Thus the sacrament strengthens and comforts the sick person in the trials and temptations against faith and hope, which he or she encounters at the approach of death. But, as this sacrament continues the healing work of Christ, it is a sign of the victory over death, which his miracles of curing the sick heralded and his resurrection has gained forever.

---

328. CCC 1520.

Chapter Seven
Ordination

The last two sacraments are known as the sacraments of mission or vocation. These are for Holy Orders and marriage. One effect of these two sacraments is that they give the recipients the grace of the *holiness* appropriate to each state of life to which the person is called, whether ordained or married. They are both directed towards the *mission* of spreading the Gospel by the example of faith and by word. These two sacraments are also directed to the *salvation* of others.[329] The priest sanctifies others by administering the sacraments to them and, in marriage, each partner sanctifies the other and, as parents, they teach the faith to their children. By preaching, the deacon or priest proclaims the word of God, to which married people bear witness by their lives in the world. Each of these two sacraments is a *consecration*, as the rite of each one makes plain. The priest obviously consecrates his life for the service of Christ, but married people too are consecrated for the duties of the married state, as it says in the prayer for the Nuptial Blessing.[330]

[handwritten marginal note: Not about self but service of others.]

---

329. CCC 1534.
330. CCC 1535. Cf. *Gaudium et Spes* 48.

The Priesthood in Scripture

Paul Haffner notes that we go back to the Old Testament for the beginning of the Christian priesthood, when the whole nation of Israel is set apart as a royal priesthood, a holy nation, at Mount Sinai (Ex 19:6). We have already seen that *all* the faithful share in the priesthood of Christ by the character they receive at their baptism. Besides the common priesthood of the faithful, there is also the special priesthood of those men who are chosen by God to serve the faithful, just as, in the Old Testament, one of the twelve tribes of Israel, the tribe of Levi, was set aside by God for providing the priests to conduct the liturgy and worship of Israel. Out of this tribe, Aaron and his sons were specially consecrated as priests (Ex 29:1-30). Seventy elders were called together by Moses, and the Spirit of God came down on them (Num 11:24-25). These elders prefigured the seventy other disciples whom Our Lord sent out after the Apostles (Lk 10:1-20). The priesthood of the Old Testament, however, was unable to fulfil its purpose, because the priests had to offer sacrifices for their own sins as well as for the sins of the people year after year (Hebr 5:3; 7:27; 10:1-4). The only person who could offer a sacrifice which would take away the sins of everyone once for all was someone who did not need to offer sacrifice for his own sins. This was Christ, who could offer the perfect sacrifice, so that no other sacrifice would need to be offered in the future (but only the same one), because he was without sin himself. He is the innocent Lamb. Christ's sacrifice is also perfect for all time because, unlike the priests of the Old Testament, he did not offer external possessions, like animals or fruits, but the greatest thing anyone could offer, namely the sacrifice of his own life. Thus Christ's priesthood is of a different kind: it was not of the Levitical order of the Old Testament, which was inherited by son from father, but of the order of Melchisedek, who appeared as from nowhere, of unknown origin (Gen 14:18; Ps 109:1; Hebr 1:1-18), just as Christ did not take his priesthood from any man. Christ's priesthood is also an *eternal* priesthood, because he rose from the dead never to die again; so he lives to intercede for us for ever (Hebr 7:25). Christ initiated the priesthood of the new order when he founded the New Covenant by pouring out his blood to sanctify the new Israel, signified by 'the cup of the new and everlasting covenant' at the Last Supper (Mt 26:28; Hebr 8:6). We see from the letter to the Hebrews that it belongs to the essence of the priesthood to offer sacrifice to God (Hebr 5:1-3). Christ is priest and sacrifice in one.

The priesthood of Christ is founded on his incarnation: he is our High Priest *as man*. It was only as man that he could offer sacrifice for our sins. Because he became man, he is able to sympathize with our weaknesses, 'tempted in every way that we are, yet without sin' (Hebr 4:15; 5:1-10). As Christ shared our humanity, though without sin, he is a merciful and compassionate High Priest and he chooses men who themselves share in human weakness to represent him as priests. In the New Covenant, however, as St Thomas Aquinas stresses, there is just *one* priest, who is Christ: 'But Christ is the fount of the whole priesthood'.[331] All validly ordained priests of the one

331. ST 3a 22, 4: *Christus autem est fons totius sacerdotii.*

Catholic Church, derive their priesthood from the one Priest, Christ. Christ himself is a priest, because the office of a priest is to mediate between men (and women) and God, and Christ is eminently the Mediator because he is God and man in one person (1 Tim 2:5). Aquinas remarks that it was not for Christ to receive the priesthood but rather *to communicate it to others*, which he first did to the Apostles.

It is clear in the Gospels that Christ passed on his authority, which he had received from the Father, to the Apostles. When he sent out the Apostles on their first mission, he commanded them to cast out devils, to heal diseases and to preach the coming of the Kingdom of God (Mt 10:1-15). St Peter was given the power to loose and bind sins (Mt 16:18). When Jesus ascended into heaven, he gave all the Apostles authority to teach and to build up the Church by baptizing (Mt 28:18-20). The Apostles were made priests at the Last Supper, when Our Lord gave them the power to renew the sacrifice of the Eucharist with the command, 'Do this as a memorial of me' as he blessed the cup (Lk 22:19). Haffner observes that the ordained ministry of the Church is of Apostolic origin: that is, it goes back to the Apostles, at the Last Supper, and did not first come from the early Christian community.[332] Herbert Vorgrimler, however, holds the opinion that a sacrament does not have to go back directly to Jesus himself for it to have been instituted by him: it is enough if its development corresponds with the words of Jesus and comes from an impulse of the Spirit. He sees the ordained priesthood

332. *The Sacramental Mystery*, p.179.

primarily as an office, but says that not all offices in the Church are found explicitly in the New Testament.[333] Vorgrimler seems to me, however, to run into difficulties, because he starts with the idea of office rather than with *the priesthood of Christ*. Colman O'Neill specifically cites Luke 22:19, quoted above, as the moment when Christ instituted the sacrament of Orders. Vorgrimler, however, agrees that Apostolic succession is essential for ordination. Haffner points out that the 'seventy others' were sent out to assist the Apostles, as priests assist bishops, who are the successors of the Apostles. The inference is that the priesthood goes back to the lifetime of Christ. The Church herself is founded on the Apostles: they are her twelve foundation stones (Eph 2:20; Rev 21:14); Christ is the corner-stone. The Council of Trent stated that, as the Church received the sacrifice of the Eucharist (at the Last Supper), there must have been a priesthood to offer it from the beginning.[334] It was only consistent of the Reformers who rejected the Mass as a sacrifice, also to deny that Christ instituted a sacrament of ordination. The Council of Trent, in reply, determined that this sacrament was instituted by 'divine command' and that the power of consecrating the Eucharist and absolving from sin was given to the Apostles.

The Development of the Sacrament

The threefold order of bishops, priests and deacons had already emerged by the end of the first century, as

---

333. *Sacramental Theology*, p.237.
334. Session XXIII (ND 1707).

this is witnessed by St Ignatius of Antioch, who was martyred circa 107.[335] The Church today recognises two degrees of participation in the priesthood of Christ: the episcopate and presbyterate. Deacons are intended to help and serve them. The term '*sacerdos*' is only used for bishops and priests, but 'all three (degrees) are conferred by a sacramental act called "ordination", that is, by the sacrament of holy orders'.[336] A bishop has no more power than an ordinary priest for consecrating the Eucharist and absolving from sin, which are the two essential powers conferred by this sacrament, but a bishop is above a priest because only a bishop can ordain new priests, and priests can only obtain permission to celebrate Mass and hear confessions from a bishop. Although priests depend on bishops for the exercise of their power, nonetheless they receive the power directly from God.[337] Bishops have the power of jurisdiction and they are in charge of the celebration of the liturgy in their own diocese. Also, only bishops are the successors of the Apostles. Vorgrimler says that bishops are for governing the Church.

Whereas bishops have often seemed to be distinguished as administrators, the Second Vatican Council taught that they receive the fullness of the sacraments of Orders: 'The holy Synod teaches that the fullness of the sacrament of Orders is conferred by Episcopal ordination'.[338] In other words, bishops are more than just superior administrators.

---

335. *Trallians* 3, 1.
336. CCC 1554.
337. Vatican II, *Presbyterorum Ordinis* 2.
338. LG 21, 2.

A sign of receiving the *fullness* of the sacrament of Orders is that, after the prayer of consecration and the laying on of hands, the oil of chrism is liberally poured over the head of the new bishop. *Lumen Gentium* goes on to say, in the same paragraph, that Tradition makes it clear that 'through the imposition of hands and the words of consecration, the grace of the Holy Spirit is given, and a sacred character is impressed, in such a way that bishops, eminently and visibly, take the place of Christ himself, teacher, shepherd and priest, and act in his person'. This passage shows us three things: first, the sacrament confers a special character, which configures the recipient to Christ Our High Priest. Secondly, holy orders equips the recipient with a special share in Christ's threefold office: as priest, who offers sacrifice; as prophet, who preaches the word of God; and as king, who rules and governs the faithful, as a shepherd. Thirdly, bishops and priests are *shepherds*. But do deacons also receive a special character through the sacrament of ordination? The Second Vatican Council was undecided on this point, but the new Catechism is quite clear that deacons also receive 'an imprint ("character") through the sacrament of Orders'.[339] Vorgrimler distinguishes the roles of bishops, priests and deacons thus: bishops and priests have the office of *mediation*, deacons the office of *service*.

The power of the Apostles was transmitted by the laying on of hands, as St Paul tells Timothy: 'Do not neglect the gift you have, which was given you by prophetic utterance when the council of elders laid their hands upon you' (1 Tim 4:14). The chief sign of the sacrament in the Middle

---

339. CCC 1570. Cf. LG 29, 1.

Ages became the handing over of the paten and chalice (*traditio instrumentorum*), but Pius XII reaffirmed that ordination is conferred by the laying on of hands alone.[340] The Holy Spirit plays the central role in the prayer of consecration. The prayer for the ordination of bishops says:

> Send down upon this chosen one the power that comes from you, the Spirit of leadership which you gave to your beloved Son Jesus Christ. He gave the Holy Spirit to the apostles, and they founded your sanctuary, the Church, everywhere on earth, to the lasting praise and glory of your Name.

For priests, we have the following prayer:

> Almighty God, we pray you: give to your servants the dignity of priesthood. Renew in them the Spirit of holiness.

And for deacons, simply:

> Send down upon them, O Lord, the Holy Spirit.

The effects of holy orders are, first, that they give 'character', which sets one apart for Christian worship, as explained in the Part I, chapter 9, on character, where the difference between the ordinary and ordained priesthood is set out.[341] This is the *res et sacramentum* of holy orders, by which the priest is configured with Christ as Priest, Prophet and King through the grace of the Holy Spirit. It also gives the grace which helps bishops to guide their flock, preach the word and sanctify others, and for priests to celebrate the Eucharist worthily.[342] This is the *res*

---

340. ND 1737 no. 4.
341. Cf. CCC 1142 and LG 10.
342. CCC 1586.

tantum or interior grace of the sacrament of Orders. We have a sacrament of Orders because, as Vorgrimler points out, the functions of preaching and leading the faithful are necessary for constituting the Church. Bishops and priests are shepherds of the flock, of which Christ is the chief Shepherd.[343] Character enables priests to act 'in the person of Christ' at Mass and in absolving from sin.

The sacrament of ordination consecrates a priest in the image of Christ, the eternal Priest, for three tasks: to preach the Gospel, to be a shepherd of the people, and to celebrate the divine worship. He exercises his sacred functions 'above all in the Eucharistic worship' when, acting in the person of Christ, he unites the prayers of the faithful to the sacrifice of Christ, who is their Head.[344] Priests co-operate with their bishop and constitute one presbyterate with their bishop, whom they make present in each local assembly. Deacons have hands laid on them 'not for the priesthood but for the ministry'. They are dedicated to the people of God in the service of the liturgy of the word (for example, a deacon always reads the Gospel when present) and of charity. A deacon has the power to baptise, bless marriages, reserve and distribute the Eucharist, preach and conduct burials.[345] Colman O'Neill observes that priests and deacons have a special aptitude for assisting their bishop in the teaching of the Faith, not because they are more gifted than lay-people but in virtue of being associated with their bishop by the

---

343. Cf. 1 Pet 5:4; Hebr 13:20.
344. LG 28, 1.
345. LG 29.

sacrament of Orders and because of their position in the Church, which possesses a hierarchy.[346] O'Neill stressed the unity of the priestly and prophetic office in Christ; Christ taught (and preached) as a priest.[347]

In its special decree on priests, *Presbyterorum Ordinis*, the Second Vatican Council first viewed the ordained priesthood within the general priesthood of all the faithful by remarking that everyone in the Church shares in the priesthood of Christ.[348] But some unite the rest into one body: these are the ordained bishops and priests. The difference between the priesthood in which all the baptised share and the ordained ministry is well brought out in *Lumen Gentium* 10, which says that Christ the High Priest, who was man, made his people a kingdom of priests. The baptised are consecrated as a holy priesthood, so that they may offer spiritual sacrifices through all their activities. All the disciples of Christ should present themselves as a sacrifice to God. The ministerial priest, by the sacred power he receives, governs the priestly people and, in the person of Christ, brings about the sacrifice of the Mass and offers it to God in the name of the people. The faithful share in the offering of the sacrifice of the Mass by virtue of their royal priesthood. (Their participation consists in uniting themselves with it.) They also exercise their priesthood by receiving the sacraments, which are part of the worship that they offer to God.[349]

---

346. Op. cit., p.101.
347. Ibid., p.157.
348. *Presbyterorum Ordinis* (henceforth PO) 2.
349. LG 10.

All the sacraments are related to the Eucharist, which contains 'the entire spiritual wealth of the Church, namely Christ himself our Pasch'.[350] All the activities of a priest 'flow from the Paschal mystery of Christ'. The priest's relation to the Eucharist is described in the same paragraph thus:

> Through the ministry of priests, the spiritual sacrifice of the faithful is completed in union with the sacrifice of Christ, the only Mediator, which in the Eucharist is offered through the priest's hands in the name of the whole Church.[351]

Priests exist to offer the sacrifice of the Mass and to forgive sins:

> However, the Lord also appointed certain men as ministers... These men held in the community of the faithful the sacred power of order, that of offering sacrifice and forgiving sins.[352]

One reason for the celibacy of priests is that those who offer the sacrifice of the Mass in the community make a visible sacrifice of their lives for this task.

Priests have first to preach the Gospel, in order to awaken faith in others and to share 'the truth of the Gospel' with them, for the people of God is first formed by hearing the word of God.[353] Priests are consecrated by God to be servants in the work of sanctifying.[354] At the Last Supper, Christ said that he had consecrated himself, so that the

---

350. PO 5.
351. PO 2,4.
352. PO 2,2. Cf. Council of Trent, Session XXIII c.1 (ND 1707).
353. PO 4.
354. PO 5.

Apostles (the first priests of the New Covenant) could be 'consecrated in truth'. He prayed: 'Sanctify them in the truth; thy word is truth. As thou didst send me into the world, so I have sent them into the world. And for their sake I consecrate myself, that they also may be consecrated in truth' (Jn 17:17-19). The first priests of the New Covenant were consecrated for the mission of the Church, to preach the Gospel of truth and so to unite those who believed into the one body of Christ, the Church. The mission of the Church derives directly from the mission which the Son received from the Father on coming into the world by his incarnation. Christ continues to exercise his eternal priesthood in the liturgy of the Church through the Holy Spirit:

> The purpose for which priests are consecrated by God … is that they should be made sharers in a special way in Christ's priesthood and, by carrying out sacred functions, act as ministers of him who through his Spirit continually exercises his priestly role for our benefit in the liturgy.[355]

We may note two things here. First, as Christ was sent by the Father, so he sent the Holy Spirit, when he returned to the Father, to enable the Church to continue the mission which he had entrusted to the Apostles. Secondly, this mission consists in making known the word of truth which Christ came to preach, and in sanctifying those who come together in the Church by believing the word of truth. Thus the liturgy, in which Christ continues to act, is an integral part of this mission. The ordained priest is a sign of Christ's presence in the liturgy of the sacraments. What makes the

---

355. PO 5.

priest the sign of Christ's presence is the 'character' which he receives through the sacrament of Orders.

Colman O'Neill says that the 'character' of holy orders makes the action of the priest a sign of the Church's worship, which shares in the worship offered by Christ as our High Priest to the Father: 'in the very act of performing such a sign, and again in virtue of his character, the minister is the symbol or sacrament of Christ at this moment acting through him'.[356] Christ could not send the Holy Spirit until he had ascended in his body to the sanctuary in heaven. The descent of the Holy Spirit on Mary, the Mother of the Church, and the Apostles at Pentecost shows us that the Holy Spirit dwells in the Church by the Apostolic succession.[357] O'Neill remarks that the Spirit is not given directly through the priest when he preaches the word, but his preaching becomes the occasion when the Spirit enters the hearts of those who hear his word. As Schillebeeckx says, the sacrament of holy orders makes a priest 'the sacramental Christ' who represents Christ to the rest of the faithful.[358] This distinguishes the ordained priesthood from the general priesthood of the people.

---

356. *Meeting Christ in the Sacraments*, p.103.
357. Ibid., p.86.
358. *Christ the Sacrament*, p.212.

Chapter Eight

Marriage

The vocation of the great majority of men and women within the Church is marriage. As the Catechism points out, the Bible begins and ends with a marriage.[359] It begins with the creation of man and woman: the woman is taken from the side of the first man and the two are to be united in one flesh (Gen 1:27; 2:21-24). Scripture ends with the wedding feast of the Lamb, which is the marriage of Christ with his Bride, the Church (Rev 19:9; 22:17). Thus the natural union of man and woman in marriage becomes a symbol of the union of Christ, the second Adam, with his Bride, the Church. As Colman O'Neill remarks, the natural complementarity of man and woman has become a new way of entering into the mystery of Christ.[360]

A Sign of God's Faithful Love

The institution of marriage was directly willed by God from the beginning of the human race. In Genesis, we read that 'God created man in his own image', 'male and female he created them' (Gen 1:27). God blessed them and told them to 'be fruitful and multiply'. The offspring of a marriage was always counted as a blessing in the Old

---

359. CCC 1602.
360. *Meeting Christ in the Sacraments*, p.237.

Testament (Ps 127:3). In the second chapter of Genesis, we are told that, when God had made all the beasts, Adam still had no fitting companion or helper; so God took a rib from his side when he was asleep and fashioned it into woman. It is because this woman was bone of his bones and flesh of his flesh that a man leaves his father and mother and 'cleaves to his wife, and they become one flesh' (Gen 2:23-24). The Fathers of the Church saw in the creation of woman from the side of Adam a figure of the birth of the Church from the side of Christ in his sleep on the Cross, when water and blood, symbolising the sacraments of baptism and the Eucharist, flowed from his side.[361] We are all born naturally in water and blood.

The union of man and woman in marriage was seen by some of the prophets as an image of God's love for Israel, who is sometimes called by them the bride of God. For example, Jeremiah said that Israel had been unfaithful to God like an unfaithful wife (Jer 3:20). Hosea announced that God was going to take back his unfaithful wife and betroth her again forever (Hos 2:19-20). Thus the prophets taught that lasting fidelity is a part of marriage. Israel was God's bride, because she had entered into a covenant with God at Mount Sinai. A covenant requires the faithfulness of both parties but, although God loved Israel with an everlasting love, Israel repeatedly failed to keep her side of the covenant. Man and woman, united in marriage, are meant to be faithful to one another, as we are meant to serve God with singleness of heart, but Israel was led astray, just as the wives of Solomon turned his

---

361. Cf. CCC 478, 766. Cf. Jn 19:34.

heart from God to other gods (1 Kgs 11:4). Divorce was allowed under the Old Law (Deut 24:1-4), but the last of the prophets made it plain that this was not part of God's plan: 'For I hate divorce, says the Lord, the God of Israel' (Mal 2:16).

Christ came to restore the original meaning of marriage (Mt 19:4-6). By appealing to Genesis 1:27 and 2:24, which he joins together, Jesus showed that the author of marriage is God. Marriage is not, therefore, a merely human institution or invention, but has divine laws, which we are not free to alter. God intended the union of husband and wife to be indissoluble; Moses only allowed divorce because of the hardness of heart of the Israelites. As Jesus remarked, it was not like that in the beginning (Mt 19:8). Faithfulness is proclaimed in the Song of Songs when it says: 'For love is as strong as death' (Sg 8:6). Vorgrimler observes that love expresses itself above all in fidelity.[362] The deepest reason why marriage is meant to be a lasting union lies in God's fidelity to his covenant with Israel and in Christ's fidelity to his Bride, the Church. Thus the sacrament of marriage gives the indissolubility first willed by God a new meaning.[363] Pope John Paul II said that the original meaning of marriage is fully revealed in Christ's sacrifice of himself on the Cross, when he showed his love for his Bride, the Church, by giving up his life for her out of love. 'The marriage of baptised persons thus becomes a real symbol of that new and eternal covenant sanctioned in the blood of Christ'.[364]

---

362. Op. cit., p.310.
363. CCC 1647.
364. *Familiaris Consortio* (henceforth FC) 13. Cf. Eph 5:25.

Why Marriage is a Sacrament

The Catechism declares that Christ raised the covenant of marriage between baptized persons to the dignity of a sacrament.[365] The Council of Trent named it as one of the seven sacraments, which were instituted by Christ, but did not say *when* Christ instituted this sacrament. That Council quoted Ephesians 5:32: 'This mystery is a profound one', and Matthew 19:6: 'So they are no longer two but one flesh. What therefore God has joined together, let not man put asunder'. It also said that marriage is part of 'the evangelical law', but it did not allude to the marriage feast of Cana as the occasion when Christ made marriage into a new sacrament.[366] The wine he made out of water on that occasion is meant to symbolise the grace of the new sacrament. Paul Haffner, however, holds that marriage was raised to the order of grace at the marriage feast in Cana.[367] The Catechism too says that 'the Church attaches great importance to Jesus' presence at the wedding of Cana. She sees in it the confirmation of the goodness of marriage and the proclamation that henceforth marriage will be the efficacious sign of Christ's presence'.[368] Marriage fulfils all three purposes of a sacrament as these were described by the Second Vatican Council: 'The purpose of the sacrament is to sanctify people, to build up the body of Christ, and, finally, to worship God'.[369]

Marriage is a sacrament, because it reflects the relation

365. CCC 1601.
366. Trent, session XXIV (ND 1806, 1807).
367. Op, cit., p.202.
368. CCC 1613. Cf. Jn 2:1-11.
369. SC 59.

between Christ and his Bride, the Church.[370] As we have noted, St Paul calls it 'a great mystery'. Although '*musterion*' in St Paul usually means God's hidden plan for salvation, it was also the word used in the early Church by Greek speakers for a sacrament, and it may have this meaning in Ephesians 5:32. Vorgrimler says that Christ's love for the Church finds its sacramental expression in the sacrament of marriage.[371] O'Neill saw it as a sacrament, because the partners enter into the *Passion of Christ*, not because of the pain that they suffer but because they reflect the love which Christ showed on the Cross.[372] This is what St Paul means when he says: 'Husbands, love your wives, as Christ loved the Church and gave himself up for her' (Eph 5:25). The union of husband and wife mirrors the union between Christ and the Church, which was particularly revealed in Christ dying for her out of love on the Cross. O'Neill also points out that marriage is a sacrament because the baptized are members of Christ's body (1 Cor 6:15-16), so the natural union of husband and wife is drawn into Christ's mystical body, the Church. In John Paul II's view, marriage was raised to a sacrament because Christ inserted it into the new and eternal covenant, of which it is a sign. 'Their [the spouses] belonging to each other is the real representation, by means of the sacramental sign, of the very relationship of Christ with the Church'.[373] This sacrament normally takes place within Mass, the

370. Eph 5:21-33.
371. Op. cit., p.309.
372. Op. cit., p.250
373. FC 13.

Catechism says, because all the sacraments are connected with the Paschal mystery of Christ, which is especially recalled in the Mass. The Mass also makes present again the sacrifice of Christ on the Cross, of which the love of husband and wife is a sign.[374] The Paschal mystery of Christ's Passion, death and resurrection, is the source of the grace of all the sacraments.[375]

The *res et sacramentum*, and so mystery of the Church, of this sacrament, was, for St Augustine, the indissoluble union of husband and wife, which reflects the bond between Christ and his Church. This union is brought about by the two spouses exchanging promises to love one another and live as husband and wife for the rest of their lives. The Church eventually established that marriage consists in the *consent* of the spouses rather than in its consummation. The Council of Florence, in 1434, taught that the efficient cause of the sacrament is the mutual consent of the spouses.[376] The Catechism says clearly: 'The Church holds the exchange of consent between the spouses to be the indispensable element that "makes the marriage"'.[377] This consent lies in the partners mutually giving themselves to each other. The consent finds its fulfilment in the two becoming one flesh. The consent must be given entirely freely on either side without any interior reservation or constraint from outside. As marriage is made by the consent, and consent is given by

---

374. CCC 1621.
375. SC 61.
376. ND 1803.
377. CCC 1626.

the spouses, it follows that the ministers of this sacrament are the bridegroom and bride themselves. In the Latin Church, ordinarily 'the spouses, as the ministers of Christ's grace, mutually confer upon each other the sacrament of Matrimony by expressing their consent before the Church'.[378] The Church is represented by the ordained minister, who conducts the ceremony or celebrates the Nuptial Mass. Through the prayer of the Nuptial Blessing, the new couple 'receive the Holy Spirit as the communion of love of Christ and the Church'.[379] The Holy Spirit is the seal of their covenant. Pope John Paul II said that the Spirit, whom Christ poured out, renders the spouses able to love one another with that charity, which Christ showed to his Bride on the Cross.[380]

Since marriage is a covenant, it is also a *contract*. Pope Leo XIII taught that sacrament and contract belong inseparably to one another in marriage. The sacrament is not a kind of adornment to a civil contract.[381] In the eyes of the Church, there is no marriage of one of her members unless he or she receives the *sacrament* of marriage. The sacrament is the contract itself, O'Neill says, because it essentially consists in the consent of the two partners.[382]

Marriage is also one of the seven sacraments, because the spouses need a *special grace* to live in the married state. We shall see what this grace is in the next section, under the effects of the sacrament.

---

378. CCC 1623.
379. CCC 1624.
380. FC 13.
381. ND 1823.
382. Op. cit., p.237.

The Effects of the Sacrament

The first effect of the sacrament, as we have seen, is the conjugal bond, because it represents the mystery of Christ's incarnation, by which human nature was wedded to divine nature, so to speak. The sacrament also represents the mystery of the new and eternal covenant. Thus it demands indissolubility and fidelity. All this is the *res et sacramentum*, because it is the mystery of the Church in this sacrament. Besides creating an indissoluble bond between the spouses, the sacrament also strengthens them and consecrates them for the duties of their married state.[383] As Haffner remarks, marriage is a sacrament because it requires a special grace to live it.[384] The grace which it gives for the daily living of marriage with all its demands and duties is the interior grace (*res tantum*) of the sacrament.

This interior grace first of all helps the spouses to attain holiness through the life they share: 'By this grace they "help one another to attain holiness in their married life and in welcoming and educating their children".'[385] John Paul II also named holiness as the first of the interior effects of the sacrament in *Familiaris Consortio*, saying that the sacrament of marriage is the source of the sanctification of Christian married couples.[386] The doctrine that each partner sanctifies the other goes back to St Paul: 'For the unbelieving husband is consecrated through his wife, and

---

383. CCC 1638. Cf. GS 48.
384. *The Sacramental Mystery*, p.200.
385. CCC 1641. Cf LG 11, 2.
386. FC 56.

the unbelieving wife is consecrated through her husband' (1 Cor 7:14). How much more then can the Christian spouses sanctify one another!

John Paul II enumerates further effects of the interior grace of a sacramental marriage. The love of the spouses is purified by the mystery of Christ's death and resurrection, which is the source of the grace of all the sacraments. They are also penetrated by the Holy Spirit, who fills them with the virtues of faith, hope and charity. Grace transforms their lives into a 'spiritual sacrifice'.[387] O'Neill said that the grace of the sacrament covers every area of married life; since it restores the interior harmony of the person. He points out that charity is the perfection of married life.[388] Love is indeed the beginning and end of everything because, as St John says, 'God is Love' (1 Jn 4:8). We are made out of love and for love: 'God who created man out of love also calls him to love – the fundamental and innate vocation of every human being. For man is created in the image and likeness of God who is himself love'.[389] The Catechism adds that the grace proper to the sacrament is intended to perfect the couple's love.[390]

The mutual giving of self to other, which expresses the love of the married couple, includes openness to children and the transmission of life. This openness to having children makes the giving of self complete and is marked by the readiness of the couple to share their love

387. FC 56.
388. Op. cit., p.248.
389. CCC 1604.
390. CCC 1641.

in the creation of new members of the family, who spring from their love and will share it in the family, which is a communion of love. 'Fecundity is a gift, an end of marriage, for conjugal love naturally tends to be fruitful'.[391] As the Catechism says, a child springs from the very heart of that mutual giving, as its fruit. By the gift of each one to the other, the spouses become co-operators with God in giving life to a new human person.[392] That marriage is ordered to the procreation and education of children, was something taught by the Second Vatican Council in *Gaudium es Spes*.[393] In the conception of a child, man and woman are involved in a work of creation, because God creates the rational soul which he infuses into the newly conceived human being and person.

The Mission of the Church

As one of the purposes of every sacrament is to build up the kingdom of God, marriage does this by giving the family a share in the *mission* of the Church. The family, John Paul II says, has the task of building up the kingdom of God.[394] The family is, in the phrase of *Lumen Gentium* 11, 'the domestic church', or the Church in miniature, for the Church is made out of families. The family reflects the Church who shows herself to be a Mother by bringing us to a new birth in the waters of baptism and by educating her children in the Faith. The Christian family is grafted

---

391. CCC 2366.
392. FC 14.
393. Gaudium et Spes 50.
394. FC 40

onto the mystery of the Church, so that it shares in the saving mission of the Church by bringing children to the sacraments of salvation. The Christian family both receives the love of Christ and communicates it to others, first within its own circle and then to families around.[395]

The Christian family also shares in the work of *evangelization*, especially in secular societies and countries with anti-Christian governments, simply by witnessing to the Christian faith and virtues. Indeed, John Paul II said that the future of evangelization in the Church depends on the family.[396] Parents are the first teachers of the Gospel to their children. The apostolic mission of the family is thus rooted in baptism, which makes us witnesses of Christ 'obliged to spread and defend the Faith by word and deed'.[397] The proclamation of the Gospel reaches its fullness in the celebration of the sacraments, by which a priestly people shares in the power of Christ the High Priest.[398] John Paul II confirmed that the ordinary priesthood of the faithful is exercised by receiving the sacraments, by prayer, and by the offering of one's life as a sacrifice.[399]

The role of the spouses in sanctifying one another through the daily living out of the sacrament of marriage reaches its highest expression in the Eucharist. 'The Eucharist is the very source of Christian marriage',[400]

---

395. FC 49.
396. FC 52.
397. LG 11, 1.
398. Cf. LG 10.
399. FC 55.
400. FC 57.

because the sacrifice of Christ that is made present in the Mass represents the covenant between Christ and the Church, of which the sacrament of marriage is the sign. For Christ sealed this Covenant in the blood of the sacrifice he offered on the Cross. This Covenant is the basis of the covenant of a sacramental marriage. As the Catechism says, 'The covenant between the spouses is integrated into God's covenant with man'.[401] The covenant which God made with Israel at Mount Sinai is fulfilled in the New Covenant, which Christ inaugurated at the Last Supper. We have already seen that marriage reflected the covenant between God and his people in the Old Testament. This relationship between God and his people, often likened by the prophets to a marriage, is now fulfilled in the relationship between Christ and his Bride, the Church.

Perhaps there is no better way of concluding this section on marriage than by quoting these words of John Paul II on the connection between marriage and the Eucharist:

> As a representation of Christ's sacrifice of love for the Church, the Eucharist is a fountain of charity.[402]

Since marriage is founded on the faithful love of two spouses, and charity is the perfection of the Christian life, it follows that marriage too can be a way of perfection. The communion of love which exists in a family is a reflection of the communion of love between the Father, Son and Holy Spirit, in the Trinity, from whom all love flows. As marriage should reflect the love which Christ showed for his Church by giving himself up for her, the sacrament

---

401. CCC 1639.
402. FC 57.

also gives the spouses a share in the Passion of Christ, from which the grace of all the sacraments derives. Thus marriage becomes the way for many to holiness, which is the vocation of everyone.

Select Bibliography

The Catechism of the Catholic Church (1992).

Durrwell, F.X., *The Resurrection*, London 1960.

Haffner, P., *The Sacramental Mystery*, Leominster 1999.

John Paul II, *Ecclesia de Eucharistia* (2003).

John Paul II, *Familiaris Consortio* (1981).

John Paul II, *Reconciliatio et Paenitentia* (1984).

Neunheuser, B., *Baptism and Confirmation*, London 1964.

O'Neill, C., *Meeting Christ in the Sacraments* (revised by R. Cessario O.P.), New York 1991.

Paul VI, *Apostolic Constitution on the Sacrament of Confirmation* (1971).

Scheeben, M., *The Mysteries of Christianity*, St Louis 1946.

Schillebeeckx, E., *Christ the Sacrament*, London, 1963.

Vatican Council II *Lumen Gentium* (1964).

Vatican Council II *Presbyterorum Ordinis* (1965).

Vatican Council II *Sacrosanctum Concilium* (1963).

Vorgrimler, H., *Sacramental Theology*, Collegeville 1992.

Yarnold, E., *The Awe-inspiring Rites of Initiation*, Edinburgh 1994.

Index